UNLEASHING THE ENERGY THAT CONNECTS US ALL

DAWN LYNN

Copyright © 2017 Dawn Lynn
All rights reserved.

Printed in the United States of America

Published by Spirit Mark Press, LLC
500 Buffalo Road, 2nd Floor, Suite 4
East Aurora, NY 14052

All rights reserved. No part of this publication may be reproduced or transmitted in any form without prior written permission of the publisher.

All examples are based on real individuals. To protect the privacy of these individuals, names and identifying details have been changed.

ISBN-13: 978-0-9990411-0-9
ISBN-10: 0-9990411-0-X

Library of Congress Control Number: 2017944365

For my daughter Tierney, may you grow up in a world where you can use your gifts openly and proudly. You have my heart.

CONTENTS

Acknowledgements   pg ix

Introduction   pg 1

Section One: Understanding the Connectedness

Chapter One:	Energy	pg 7
Chapter Two:	The Intuitive	pg 14
Chapter Three:	Physical Intuition	pg 19
Chapter Four:	Emotional Intuition	pg 31
Chapter Five:	Spiritual Intuition	pg 50

Section Two: Getting the Messages

Chapter Six:	What Happens When You Use Your Intuition	pg 63
Chapter Seven:	Fear of Intuition	pg 77
Chapter Eight:	How the Messages Come	pg 92
Chapter Nine:	Helping You Achieve Your Life's Purpose	pg 103

Section Three: Working with the Universe

Chapter Ten:	Trust	pg 115
Chapter Eleven:	Ego	pg 123
Chapter Twelve:	Respect	pg 140
Chapter Thirteen:	Gratitude	pg 148
Chapter Fourteen:	Patience	pg 157

Epilogue   pg 161

Appendix   pg 163

References   pg 168

Index   pg 169

ACKNOWLEDGMENTS

There are so many people who have helped make this book possible. So many in fact, that I could write a whole book in gratitude. But these are a few folks who truly went above and beyond.

Starting with my family, I want to thank my mom and dad. You have always supported me in my crazy endeavors and made me believe anything is possible. And you know what? You were right. With a little, and sometimes a lot, of hard work, I have been able to accomplish anything I put my mind to. Who would have thought? I've written a book!

To my Aunt Vickey, you have always been like a mother to me and now a "nana" to my daughter. Thank you not only for the emotional support you've provided throughout the years but also the constant helping hand. You've always been there. Thank you!

To Terry and Barry, as stepparents you have both always been supportive of my career, which I'm sure wasn't easy. Who dreams about having a medium as a stepdaughter? You both have gone above and beyond, especially as I worked on this book. Barry, you sought out and gifted me tools and resources that I wouldn't have gotten myself. The knowledge provided insight that made this book a reality. And Terry, thank you for taking the time to not only proofread the first draft but always keeping up on what I'm doing.

Speaking of proofreaders, thank you Jen Holliday, Sue Drozd-Kowalski and Ginny Sukmanowski for plowing through the rough first draft. Not only were your edits helpful, but you affirmed that the book was worthwhile. I needed that support to keep moving forward.

To bring the book to actuality, I need to thank my copy editor Carole Knuth; my cover designer, Joe Babcock; and party planner extraordinaire, Cassandra Boyd. You all made me look like I knew what I was doing. Thank you!

Last but not least, I have to thank my husband, Don. Where do I begin? There is so much to say and yet, I'll keep it short. This book wouldn't be here if it weren't for you. I don't know what I would do without you. Thank you for being my rock. I love you.

INTRODUCTION

Do you consider yourself "spiritual, but not religious"?

If so, you are not alone. This ideology is growing within the United States. According to the Pew Research Center, in 2012 the percentage of Americans who did not identify with any religion bounced up to 20% from 15% in 2007.[1] That number is even greater among Millennials at 34%![1]

But what does "spiritual, but not religious" mean?

If you are like me, you believe in something bigger than yourself but don't see the need for, or perhaps don't care for, organized religion. Because of this belief, you are likely seeking a greater understanding of yourself and the universe. Perhaps that's why you picked up this book and have read others. Sorry to disappoint you, but it is unlikely the answers you seek will be contained within this or any book. Rather you will find the answers through intuition.

That doesn't mean reading is a futile exercise, however. Books can guide you to your intuition. In fact, that's why I wrote this book. As a medium, I get asked by numerous people if they too have the "gift." My answer to each and every single one of them is, "Of course you are intuitive. Everyone is!" Some smile and walk away taller. Others look at me like I'm crazy. Either way, it gets them

ONE

thinking and wondering, "What exactly does it mean to be intuitive"?

The reason they wonder about intuition is because the term is thrown around by celebrities, TV personalities, news broadcasters, and even scientists. It has become a catchphrase. And, for the spiritual, but not religious folks, it conjures thoughts of being able to find their inner knowing and spirituality. Unfortunately, as a catchphrase the concept of intuition changes from person to person. If you were to ask five people to define intuition, you would likely get five different answers.

Without a clear definition of what intuition is, for some it brings fear. That fear could stem from their family's belief system. Or it might be a result of negative depictions of the paranormal in the media. Or there could be personal experiences from the past that were frightening. Or there may even just be a fear of the unknown. Whatever the case may be, the lack of clarity around what intuition is can be daunting.

So, before we go any further, let's clear up what intuition is, at least within the pages of this book. To do that, I'm going to start with what intuition isn't. Intuition isn't limited to receiving messages from your long-deceased Great Aunt Ida. Nor is it just about communicating with a friend's deceased parent to bring your friend comfort. That is mediumship. Additionally, intuition and psychic should not be used synonymously. Intuition is not limited to knowing or being able to predict the future for yourself or others.

Don't mistake this for saying that mediumship and psychic are not forms of intuition, because they are. But you can choose to not be a medium or psychic and still be intuitive. Intuition, at least as defined by me in this book, is much broader than either of these. In this book, intuition is defined as the instinctive knowing that comes without any rhyme or reason why. Not only that, it is

INTRODUCTION

about observing and creating a connection with the world around you. It is trusting your instincts on a physical, emotional and spiritual level. And, most importantly, it is about acting upon the information you have received.

Why would you be interested in using your intuition? If you are one of those spiritual, but not religious folks, it helps you better understand the world around you and yourself. By observing and intuiting the environment around you, you become more aware and informed. With additional information upon which to base life decisions, it is easier to make tough decisions. Additionally, because you have more information upon which to make decisions, you tend to make better decisions, resulting in fewer obstacles and less heartache. Does this mean life becomes easy? No. Life is not easy, never will be, but it does become easier. Not only that, you will have a confidence in the direction you are going, resulting in a greater inner peace and hope. Who doesn't want that? And if I can teach you that, I am one happy camper. As mentioned earlier, I wholeheartedly believe that everyone is intuitive. I also believe intuition is the path to peace, joy and happiness.

Why do I believe cultivating your intuition will bring joy? Simply put, I have witnessed it in my friends, my family, in strangers and I have lived it. From little things like getting help from the universe in finding a parking spot on a rainy day to the universe bringing the right people into my life at the right time (such as a contractor or realtor) to assisting me in accomplishing my life purpose by providing me with means, the universe has always been there when I needed it. And my life has always changed for the better.

I've felt "lucky." This is a feeling I want everyone to have and which has inspired me to share my knowledge with the world. It is my life goal to normalize intuition. I don't want to simply tell people what I see, I want to teach

ONE

them how to see for themselves. I want to help you cultivate your intuition.

Intuition will give you that little bit of "luck" when bad things happen. You will realize you are not alone. Just as in the famous poem *Footprints*, the universe carries you through the hard times. Knowing this helps you approach negative situations with hope, not fear.

I hope you find as much enjoyment reading this book as I had writing it. Let's get started.

SECTION ONE
UNDERSTANDING THE CONNECTEDNESS

CHAPTER ONE
ENERGY

"If you want to find the secrets of the universe, think in terms of energy, frequency and vibration."
Nikola Tesla

Energy. It is a catchphrase that new age, metaphysical and spiritual individuals throw around a lot. You've probably heard comments like "My energy is off today" or "That person has bad energy". Statements like these are common because everyone feels energy. When people begin to awaken their intuition, the impact and sensation of those energies are recognized to a greater degree. Thus, a conversation about intuition would be incomplete without first addressing the topic of energy.

What is energy? Energy is like gravity. It is unseen and it impacts every single one of our actions. Like gravity, which allows us to walk, run, and stay firmly planted on earth, not floating off into space, energy is an electromagnetic force we all emit that affects our interactions with others. It is also the force that allows intuition to be possible. Unfortunately, like gravity, while most individuals acknowledge that energy exists and that it affects them, they do not have a clear understanding of how or why it works. To begin our discussion, let's explore the hows and whys of energy.

ONE

Scientifically, energy is explained by basic physics. In physics, there is the assertion that all objects – you, me, a parrot, a chair, a rock, a tree, the air you breathe, everything – are composed of atoms. Atoms are the basic building blocks of existence that, when cobbled together, create the world in which we live. Because everything, including the air, is full of atoms, empty space is an illusion. Rather, we are in physical contact with the world around us at all times.

Being in continuous contact with all aspects of the world, every movement, no matter how slight, has an effect. Those effects can be anticipated, such as the nod of acknowledgement you receive when placing your hand on a friend's shoulder to alert him of your presence at a party. Getting your friend's attention was the anticipated outcome, but there are often unanticipated effects as well. In the scenario discussed, you've just touched your friend's shoulder. As you do, another party-goer gives you a jarring shove. This was unanticipated because unbeknownst to you, you created a bottleneck in movement and the party-goer was moving too fast to stop. Those unexpected reactions are what physicists call the butterfly effect. The premise of this theory is that small changes, such as the flapping of butterfly wings in North America can create large changes elsewhere, such as a tsunami in southeast Asia. Does it always? No. Could it? Yes.

It's important to note that disruption to energy is not limited to movements created by our physical body. Subtle shifts in your emotions and thoughts can also create significant impacts to your environment. Have you ever noticed that a shift in your attitude or thoughts creates change? For example, it's been a tough few weeks. Desiring change, you wake up and tell yourself that it is going to be a good day. To your surprise, it is. So is the next and the next. Why is this?

Emotions and thoughts are energy. As energy, they have their own unique vibrations. These vibrations are similar to the frequencies of light and sound. Just because you don't see the movement of sound or light doesn't mean it doesn't exist or can't be measured. Most importantly, just because you don't see the waves of energy doesn't mean it doesn't have an impact on you. Think about when a dog trainer blows a dog whistle. You know the whistle is making a sound because your dog responds, but because the pitch is outside of human range you don't audibly hear it. Because you do not hear it, you are likely not conscious of the sound's impact on you. At least not right away. If the trainer continues to blow the whistle, you may end up with a headache. This is a demonstrable outcome from the unseen force.

Similarly, comprehension or consequences of the unseen energetic vibrations of thoughts and feelings surrounding us are often noticeable. For example, an individual often doesn't have to say a word for you to instinctively know his or her mood. This may be perceived through body language, but the knowing may also be a feeling you get. When you get that intuitive feeling, you are likely to respond accordingly. For example, your boss appears to be in a bad mood. You may respond by either avoiding or trying to cheer him or her up.

Situations like that happen multiple times every day, but if your senses of sight and sound aren't providing you with information on what's wrong, how is it that you know? How is it that you respond appropriately?

Let's return to the concept of atoms. It has been established that everything is comprised of atoms. Did you know that each atom has a unique size, weight, and like magnets, positive and negative charge? They do! Due to these factors, each atom vibrates at its own unique frequency. These frequencies, or forces of energy, are much like notes in music. For example, the note A has a different tone, wavelength and vibration than the note C. Similarly, a calm and mellow individual has a different energy than an anxious and determined one.

The similarities and differences between frequencies explain why you can meet a stranger and get along beautifully, and yet you avoid your kind uncle like the plague because you have little in common. Atoms of similar frequencies attract one another. Like atoms, similar energies are attracted to one another while those that are dissimilar repel.

Because we tend to surround ourselves with similar energies, we become accustomed to the frequencies of the energy around us. When a circumstance is off kilter, as observers we become aware of the imbalance. For example, when a new musician joins a band, he or she may play slightly flat or sharp in comparison to the rest of the band. The entire band is acutely aware of this difference and the sound can be ear shattering on both a physical and energetic level.

In physics, atoms will undergo reactions to become as neutral and stable as possible. Atoms do not like to be energetically unstable. An example of this is hydrogen peroxide. Hydrogen peroxide, H_2O_2, is water with an extra oxygen attached. The extra oxygen causes this compound to be more reactive than water and is the reason it is great at taking out stains. Due to its instability, hydrogen peroxide is packaged in dark containers, for when left in a clear glass container, it will break down to water and oxygen, two stable compounds.

Energetically, humans aren't much different. We seek stability. We accomplish the desired stability and balance through compromise. Continuing the example of the off-key musician, the insertion of this musician has shaken things up. To adjust to this, he and everyone in the band will adjust their key to bring a harmony. It is how we adapt.

The trend towards neutrality is one way energy impacts us. Gravitational pull, one of the four fundamental forces in physics, is another. The concept of gravitational pulls is that objects with greater mass and density exert a stronger pull than objects with lesser mass and density. Additionally, objects in closer proximity to one another have a greater impact on one another than objects at greater distances. For example, a spouse with whom you live is likely to have a greater impact on your day to day choices than a parent who lives states away. You and your spouse are together every day, so not only are you in closer proximity, you are more likely to understand your spouse's hopes and dreams and witness his or her disappointment, which will drive you to appease your spouse more than your parent. However, if your parent is oppressive and judgmental or if you have not freed yourself from said parent, you may seek his or her approval to such a degree that you respond to parental requests as opposed to your spouse's. In this scenario, despite your spouse being in closer proximity, the denseness of your parent's opinion will exert a stronger pull.

And that, folks, is the basic science behind how energy works. To summarize:
- Everything is made of atoms and frequencies.
- Empty space is an illusion.
- We are always in physical contact with the world around us.
- Slight shifts, including those in thoughts and feelings, create change.
- The closer the proximity or the stronger the pull, the greater the shift.
- Energy wants to move to stability and balance.

ONE

With that in mind, let's explore how energy could impact you on an ordinary day.

It is 8:00 am and you are sitting on a crowded bus going to work. You are happy to have a seat, even if it means you are squashed next to a window with a sizable person on your left. Due to the crowded nature of the bus, you aren't surprised to feel the movements (or energy) of the person next to you. You feel when he shifts in his seat as well as the movements he makes each time he turns a page of his newspaper. Your ear drum is pierced by the screaming toddler sitting somewhere in the back. Your phone rings and as you squirm to answer it, you hear (and perhaps feel) an annoyed, heavy sigh from your seat mate. Not only that, you feel a jolt to your seat when a person from the back shuffles past your row on the way off the bus.

In this scenario, you are just one small part (one atom). All the other players, from the person next to you to the baby crying to your ringing phone and the man scurrying to get off the bus are other atoms. As one changes, you are impacted. That's energy.

In life, as in the example, you are just one of many small components. A passive participant will respond, without even knowing it, to the surrounding energies. In this example, you accommodated the sizable man sitting beside you by squishing yourself against the window. After hearing the heavy sigh of annoyance, again you accommodated by speaking more quickly and quietly to the person on the phone. And, lastly, you readjusted yourself after receiving the jolt from the individual passing you by. You responded to the energies around you. That's basic physics, not intuition.

How, then, can the basics of physics be used to facilitate intuition?

It is quite simple. You shift from a passive participant to an active, observant one. As an active participant, you respond to the circumstances around you. Not only that, you affect the outcome. As an active participant, through purposeful and deliberate action, the energy you emit assists in obtaining desirable outcomes. To be purposeful in your actions, you must be aware of your surroundings. That awareness is your intuition.

Let's go back to the example of the bus. An intuitive individual might hear the person shuffling from the back of the bus and turn around. At that point, the intuitive might notice the hastiness or clumsiness of the passenger moving forward as well as the grimaces and grumbles of the people as the passenger passes by them. These outward signs may lead the intuitive to reason that the passenger is disrupting his surroundings. As a result, when the passenger nears the row of seats, the intuitive is prepared and braces for a jolt. Less startled and prepared, the intuitive's comfort is not disturbed.

That's how energy and intuition work together. Energy is the slight movements in a scenario that indicate a situation will go one way. Intuition is the perception of those shifts that prepare you for the outcome. You may be thinking that there is nothing special about that. That's just an individual being observant. You are correct! There is nothing special about it. The intuitive is the observer. Anyone can do it.

ONE

CHAPTER TWO
THE INTUITIVE

"The intuitive mind is a sacred gift and the rational mind is the faithful servant. We have created a society that honors the servant and has forgotten the gift."
Albert Einstein

Since the intuitive is simply the observer, it comes to reason that everybody is intuitive. Everyone is. If you are thinking you are not, throw that thought right out the window. In fact, it is likely you are already using your intuition every day. Remember, intuition is not limited to mediumship or psychic phenomenon, it is more broadly the ability of being perceptive of the subtle shifts in the energies or circumstances around you.

Let's look at ways your intuition could be showing itself. You might be admiring a "glow" around your friend, only to then notice she is avoiding alcohol. These observations lead you to believe she is pregnant. Or your intuition could cause you to bite your tongue in a meeting with your boss because you can tell from his or her tone, circles around the eyes and a frazzled look that being overwhelmed is a problem. Upon coming to this conclusion, you postpone submitting a request for time off, believing it would be more warmly received at a future time. Or perhaps you run into a husband and wife, they are smiling, standing hand-in-hand and laughing together. Upon observing the interaction, you get a feeling in the pit of your stomach and know, despite any outward signs, that he is cheating. Two months later you find out you are correct. Your intuition may also be communicating with you if you have ever found yourself procrastinating, only to find when you do finally tackle the task that circumstances have changed and by procrastinating you have saved yourself work. Or you decide to take a trip and while researching options look at a travel website you don't normally book through and you find an amazing deal. I could go on and on. The examples are endless. And as you can tell, they aren't that out of the ordinary. One or many of these examples may have happened to you.

Situations like those outlined above happen daily to everyone. Why? Because the energies that create these circumstances impact everyone. Energy, which facilitates intuition, doesn't discriminate or hide information from anyone. It's not like in a courtroom where one lawyer has information and withholds it from the other, only to surprise the other in the middle of the case in hopes of gaining an upper hand. Energy doesn't want an upper hand. Unlike in a courtroom, energy isn't looking for a winner or a loser. Everyone is on the same side. As discussed in the previous chapter, energy seeks balance.

The question, then is, how often do you dismiss these feelings? If you are like most people, frequently. If you are dismissing these energies, you probably don't feel intuitive. Don't be discouraged. Although intuition is deemed a "gift," the only reason one individual is more intuitive than another is how closely surrounding energies or circumstances are observed and then how one applies the observations to actions.

Let's apply this concept to the example of the friend that you assumed was pregnant. Assuming you observed her in approximately the same physical state as her other friends and colleagues would see her, the more observant, intuitive friends would notice the "glow." The others would not. The intuitives would assume, and perhaps explore and debunk, the idea that the friend didn't have the glow as a result of lathering herself up with oil. The non-intuitives didn't notice the glow and so there is no need to determine where it is from. The intuitives would continue looking for details to support their pregnancy assumption and notice she is avoiding alcohol like you did, or they might notice she went to the bathroom more, drank more water and avoided caffeine. When presented with all the same facts, the intuitives will notice these actions and intuit she is pregnant. The unobservant will not. They do not notice the subtle differences.

This is no different than a novice and artist when it comes to colors. A layman may be able to distinguish the difference between green and purple but may not know the difference between chartreuse and lime green or violet and amethyst. However, an artist would, just as the intuitive observes the nuances of behavior.

As an individual becomes more sensitive and intuitive, he or she shifts from being a passive observer of energy to an active participant in the world. As noted above, the intuitive drew conclusions along the way, often also making minor adjustments to any actions so as to maintain balance and avoid becoming drastically out of sync with the immediate environment. For example, the intuitive friend of the pregnant woman may be mindful not to order seafood or spritz themselves with perfume after going to the bathroom. Minor shifts allow the active participant to steer energy towards the highest and best. By doing this, the intuitive often feels empowered and experiences higher self-esteem than the non-intuitive.

An example of an intuitive individual adapting

behavior to create impactful change can be demonstrated by the actions of Millie, a woman I knew. Millie was a phenomenal executive director and community leader. Part of her success could be attributed to her intuition. Not only was Millie sensitive to energy, she also utilized that intuition daily. She leaned on it to assist her in understanding her community and the organizations she partnered with. She listened with her heart to hear her partners' words. Only after they had finished speaking would she craft a response. Because she was fully engaged in what her partners were saying, she observed the subtle energies of her partners' words and actions. These energies provided her with a solid understanding of the driving forces behind the individuals and their respective organizations. With this understanding, she navigated sticky terrain.

    Millie understood we are all connected. From that came her unwavering belief that for her to be successful, her partners had to be successful. With each step, she insisted her partners' needs were met. By doing this, she brought people and organizations, that didn't typically collaborate, together. With all parties at the table, she was the catalyst to significant change within the community. Had Millie not trusted her gut and read the signs around her, she would not have had the success she did.

    The use of her intuition not only assisted her in creating balance and maximizing the resources of her community; Millie often found herself in the right place at the right time. To seemingly always be in the right places at the right time is another attribute of intuition.

    Let's explore an example of being in the right place at the right time. A few years ago, my friends and I had tickets to a comedy show. We went downtown and planned on getting a bite to eat beforehand. Because traffic was heavy, we ended up getting downtown later than expected. Due to time restraints, rather than going to a brewery, assuming it would be quicker, we hit the chain that was right down the street from the theater. Favoring local restaurants, this would never have been my choice, but that afternoon it proved to be fortunate. Turns out, the comedian we had tickets to see was sitting in the booth next to us. This gave us a once in a lifetime opportunity. Not only did we get autographs, we got a few laughs.

Intuitives frequently seem to be in the right place at the right time. As a result, they have the best and sometimes unbelievable stories. Why? An intuitive follows gut instincts and is attuned to noticing patterns, trends and synchronicities the naked eye may not necessarily see. Not only will an intuitive recognize trends before others do, but will often seize those opportunities as opposed to letting them pass by. It is important to note, much of this recognition occurs subconsciously. The conscious mind may have no awareness of the nuances that drive its actions.

Trends are all around us, from the stock market to fashion. As the pendulum swings and one trend falls out of favor to make way for something shiny and new, being able to anticipate the shape of the shiny and new is a skill of intuitives. By utilizing their past experiences, observations from society and that indescribable gut feeling, they walk the spider web and get a sense of the next trend.

In order to understand how intuitives utilize their intuition to create informed opinions, let's look at the various types of intuition.

CHAPTER THREE
PHYSICAL INTUITION

"Instinct guides the animal better than the man. In the animal it is pure, in man it is led astray by his reason and intelligence."
Denis Dierdot

The first type of intuition we will discuss is physical intuition or primal instincts. Humans, due to their ability to modify and control their environment, sometimes forget we are, at our root, the animal named *homo sapiens*. Animals have an instinctive ability to connect with nature. If you have ever taken the opportunity to watch animals in the wild, you know they have an uncanny ability to sense the presence of prey or a predator. They also have an ability to blend in with their environment, concealing their presence from would-be prey or predators. These abilities are facilitated by heightened senses of sight, smell and sound. Some animals are equipped with senses outside the human spectrum, like bats and whales that use echolocation. Wild animals rely on these senses heavily, for awareness of their environment is a matter of life and death.

Humans were once equipped with the ability to read the environment like our animal brethren. As humans have evolved and become greedy, the ability to use their instincts led to the extinction of wildlife and destruction of natural environments. In a Celtic parable, it is suggested that to balance the scales and preserve our natural environment, father sky and mother earth stripped humans of their instinctual ability to read their environment, leaving them with limited natural instincts.

    The moral and truth of this tale can be observed in western industrialized society. We take what we want as we strive to "get rich," regardless of the impact on the environment. This is seen in the western United States where gold, silver and copper were mined only to be abandoned and cause ecological hazards. The burning of coal and other emissions has impacted the air we breathe. The examples are endless. Not only that, in the industrialized world, humans have elevated themselves to the top of the food chain. Humans don't have nor do they fear a natural predator. Without a predator that at any moment could take one's life, there is a sense of security. Due to this sense of safety, many individuals have stopped utilizing, or perhaps as the parable states, lost, their instinctive reflexes and senses. This is especially true in suburban and urban society. As a result, many humans are unobservant and ignorant of the world around them. Additionally, the less these senses are utilized, the weaker the muscle becomes. Humans become further disconnected from their natural environment. It's a downward spiral.

    This skill is not lost, however. We were once those wild animals. Like wild animals, the ability to perceive the environment still exists within us. All you must do is pay attention to the environment. Consider for a moment how much more vivid sound becomes in a quiet room. A pin drop that would be lost in the noise of a busy street can be deafening. Personally, I experienced this after a severe car accident from which I lost my peripheral vision. Having tunnel vision was challenging at first. I startled easily. In stores, people would step up beside me to look at an item, but not seeing them, I would turn and bump into them. Similarly, in restaurants a server would come with food and, if I couldn't see him coming, I would jump as the plate was placed in front of me. Over time, while my vision hasn't improved, my hearing, as well as my ability to sense a person's presence, has. We adapt. If we want to, that is.

What makes an individual want to adapt? As king of our environment and without a natural enemy, many individuals aren't afraid of being eaten by a tiger or going hungry because we don't know where or how to forage for food. Thus, fear for our safety isn't causing us to want to adapt and become more in tune with our environment. Or could it?

Let's talk cell phone usage. No matter where you go, there are individuals whose attention is focused not on their environment, but rather, on their smart phone. The preoccupation with smart devices over other activities has resulted in law-makers having discussions around distracted driving and even distracted walking. These conversations are not only appropriate but necessary as the dangers distracted individuals pose are very real. Don't think so? Take a moment to think about your last trip to the grocery store. How often did you see an individual pushing a cart with their nose in a smart phone? How many times did someone doing that bump into you? Or did you see them bump into someone else? I know I've been bumped into more than one. These individuals' preoccupation with their device has left them with no awareness of the people or environment around them.

The bumps and bruises caused to you and your fellow man due to the lack of awareness of the physical environment can be devastating. In 2015 alone, over

391,000 individuals were injured in motor vehicle accidents involving distracted drivers according to the United States Department of Transportation and the National Highway Safety Association.[2] That's a lot of hurt people as well as a good reason to be more connected to your environment.

These injuries, however, are minor in comparison to another harm occurring. Your physical connection to the world around you, inclusive of your community and environment, is being disrupted. This disruption can cause you to be energetically out of whack, ungrounded and disconnected. If not connected to your environment, you may experience depression, apathy, lethargy, anxiety as well as hopelessness.

How can your physical connection to your environment help with this? The natural environment helps you understand your place, which sets the foundation for understanding your life purpose. Understanding your place can create a sense of security and comfort which promotes a sense of well-being and happiness.

Additionally, nature has an ability to remove excess energy and calm an individual. Think about the last time you were by water or surrounded by trees. It may even have been in a city where cars and people were whistling past you. Did you find your tensions and stresses wash away only to be replaced with a peace and serenity? Most likely.

Why does this happen? As mentioned in the discussion about energy, energies trend towards stabilization and balance. Nature, a powerful force like the steady beats of percussion in an orchestra, has a way of forcing you to vibrate at its level. Fortunately, the vibration of nature while massive and steadfast, is gentle and calming. Not only that, nature's vibration is that of a human's natural state. By being in your natural environment, the disruption created by the technological, fast-paced world within which we live is minimized, if not altogether eliminated. Amazingly, it only takes a few moments to bring someone back to their natural state.

As referenced above, there are a few aspects of the modern society that inhibit our instinctual intuition and cause us to be out of sync with the natural environment. The first is our manufactured environment. The second is that most of us are constantly in motion. The combination of the two leaves individuals feeling stressed and without a sense of place in this great big world. Let's talk about why that is.

In the United States, approximately 80 percent of the population lives in urban areas.[3] For individuals residing in urban areas, materials like concrete, steel and plastic are everywhere they go. Concrete is used in construction because it is strong and practically indestructible. Energetically, it is the same. Its atoms vibrate slowly, are rigid and unbending. Concrete acts as a barrier and does not absorb energy like nature does. Rather, it acts like a cage for the frenzied energy we create in our lifestyle.

In our manufactured, modernized world, a portion of the frenzied energy is a result of technology. Cell phones, televisions, computers and the internet all emit electromagnetic waves. While these electromagnetic waves are not visible, they influence everyone, even an individual that does not personally own or use these devices. How do they influence everyone? Frequencies are being emitted from towers to facilitate the sharing of data over the airways. These frequencies not only hit the devices meant to capture the information, but they also hit and are absorbed by you. The impact may be minimal, but it exists. Don't believe me? If there is a power plant nearby, go and visit it. If not, find a location with multiple power towers and stand in the towers' shadow. Pay attention to how you feel. It is not uncommon for individuals to experience headaches, have a taste of metal in their mouths, and ringing in their ears.[4] The energy has an effect.

The closer you live to a power station or generator, the greater effect it will have. The number of electronic devices you own will also impact you. More devices, more impact. Why? Each device not only accepts the electromagnetic frequencies but also emits them. The emission of energy serves as a beacon to attract the frequencies emitted from a power tower. The emission of that energy has an impact on you and your environment.

Not only that, consider where these devices are usually located. Chances are it is in close proximity to you, be it in your pocket, purse, desk top, or even in bed. Due to the nearness, the frequencies of these devices impact you twenty-four hours, seven days a week. The frequencies which are usually between 10 and 300 hertz[4] are not in resonance with a human's natural state of 10 hertz.[5] Going back to the basic physics, it is logical that your body will respond by speeding up your vibration to align with that of the forces around you. This scattering of energies is often disruptive. My husband and I noticed this in our daughter. At about a year and a half, she suddenly started having disrupted sleep. We ruled out illness, growing pains, temperature, noise, as well as many other potential reasons, but her sleep remained disrupted. Running out of options, my husband mentioned the wireless internet router located in her room as a potential source. Willing to try anything, we removed it from her room. Immediately we witnessed a shift. Within a week, her sleep pattern resumed. The frequencies emitted by the router were obviously affecting her. Unlike materials like concrete and plastics that are unbending, these electromagnetic waves emit a strong pull and force energies to change. The influence of technology is particularly troubling as many individuals don't recognize the influence.

Materials like concrete and plastics as well as technology are becoming more and more prevalent, replacing and destroying our natural environment. This makes it hard for nature to compete.

But that's just one aspect of the problem; the other is an individual's bustling lifestyle. Many individuals find themselves in continuous movement. Constantly on the go, your energy does not stay put long enough for you to become aware of or adjust to your environment. Without time, nature does not have the opportunity to assert its influence.

Fortunately, due to the power of nature, you don't need a lot of time to connect with it. Creating a connection is as simple as walking barefoot in the grass, or sitting outside on the balcony soaking up the sun and feeling the wind in your hair. Unable to go outside? Try taking a bath and immersing yourself in water, especially if you have some Epsom salts. Even that can do the trick. Whatever it is, do it. In fact, make a habit of connecting with nature.

Why? Connecting with nature is the first step to utilizing your physical intuition. How does it assist you in utilizing your instincts? It brings you to your natural energetic state. This is important because in your natural state you are more likely to be observant of your surroundings and productively engage in your environment. For example, as deadlines for this book approached, I found myself stressed and preoccupied with my to-do list. My energy was scattered. Being scattered, I didn't realize how far I had come and the opportunities that aligned for me. Only after I paused and my energy settled did I connect.

Connecting with nature is a great tool because it is simple. The next step to awakening your physical intuition is easy as well. All it takes is focused intention and time. In this step, pause and become observant of your surroundings. Let's practice right now.

Exercise 1
Getting In Touch With Your Environment

Sit back and get comfortable. Take a moment to look around the room you are in. Don't just glance at your surroundings. Study the intricate details of the space. Notice the colors that surround you and the way light creates shadows. Take a moment to notice the details of the objects. Notice the number of items and their placement. Examine the environment on such an intricate level that you notice the flaws, such as a rhinestone that may be missing from a picture frame or a knot in the wood paneling that appears to form a face. See the beauty in those flaws. Sit and just look around your environment.

After absorbing the sights of your environment, complete the exercise for sounds, touch and smell. In a mere five minutes, you will be surprised by the intricacies you never noticed before. Imagine what you will see in ten or twenty!

What did you notice that you didn't notice before? How did you feel while going through the exercise? You may have experienced your senses being heightened. Colors seemed brighter. Perhaps you noticed the differences between lilac and amethyst, or, a peace and calm may have washed over you. You may even have felt at one with your environment. Take the time to complete this exercise a couple of times in different environments. Once you do, it will become second nature. Don't be surprised to find yourself walking into rooms and immediately taking stock of everything.

The previous exercise assists you in becoming observant of the sight, sound, touch and smell of your environment. This is useful in awakening your intuition because paying attention to the details allows you to observe when something is different. But these observations are limited to that which can be experienced with the five senses. As we know from the discussion about energy, the environment is composed of much that we are unable to see, hear, touch, taste and feel. How can you perceive that energy?

Worried that it is going to be hard? Don't fret. Chances are, you are already observing that unseen energy. Don't believe me? Have you ever had goosebumps or had the hair stand up on the back of your neck? Felt like someone was watching you? Or had a peer point a finger at you and tease, "I'm not touching you!" and you'd swear they were. What about when you completed the previous exercise? Did you have feelings that you couldn't explain? These are all examples of physical intuition and perception through your energetic, or auric, field.

What is an auric field or aura? It is the energetic field that surrounds and is radiated by you. As mentioned previously, you, like your electronic devices, send out energy. It is your energetic signature. And, although it is relatively constant, with your mood, this energy goes up and goes down.

You have probably felt the auras of your friends. Think for a moment of the energy, often seen through personality traits, of your mother. Now think of your best friend. Their energies are probably very different. Now just think of your mother. Think of her happy, then frustrated. Again, different. But this time, there were probably similarities. Those similarities are the person's aura.

That aura is emitted, but also, like electronic devices, it receives energy. The receptive nature of the aura is why when someone pretends to touch you and is not, even though you think he or she is. Through the aura, you become perceptive of the invisible forces in your environment. Why? Because your energetic field, not being solid, is closer in frequency to other unseen vibrations. Remember, like attracts like!

Let's take a moment to explore awakening the auric field.

Exercise 2
Perceiving the Energy of Your Environment
This exercise is best practiced with a friend.

Start by closing your eyes or blindfolding yourself. Get comfortable in your seat. Take three deep, rhythmic breaths in and out. Rub your hands together until they are warm and tingle. Take another few deep breaths. Allow the tingling and warmth felt in your hands to move through your arms to your torso. From there feel it move up to your face and finally down your legs to your feet.

Without moving a limb, envision your hands stretching out to the world around you. If doing this exercise with a friend, have your friend point a finger at different points of your body. The finger should be two to six inches from your body. Once positioned, have your friend ask you where the finger is. If you aren't sure, ask that intention be focused on the place of your body. Have your friend do this at several different points of your body. Don't be discouraged if you get it wrong! Keep trying!

Next, ask your friend to place objects from the room in front of you. Don't touch the object; rather, use your energy to reach out and wrap itself around the object. Only then should your friend start interacting with the object. For example, if it is a fan, turn it on. If an apple, the friend should eat it. Eyes closed, use your sense of sound, smell and feeling, not touch, to observe the environment and express all your feel.

Finally, have your friend walk you around the room blindfolded. Before starting, have your friend create an obstacle course for you to navigate. Chairs and tables may be moved or cushions and objects may be placed around the room for you to find. Your friend is only there for protection, not to lead you.

If alone, place several items on a table in front of you. With eyes closed, reach out to them. Envision yourself interacting with them. Take note on how you visualize that environment and what different sensations you feel. For example, you have both an apple and banana in front of you. You notice that when you hold the apple it feels much heavier than the banana, even though you know they are the same weight. Pay attention to those subtle energetic cues.

If alone, if you are gutsy, you can stand up, spin yourself and then walk around the room. If you are not comfortable doing this, envision yourself walking around the room. Notice if corners feel denser or warmer. Notice all the details.

This exercise can also be done in a public venue. Sit upon a bench and close your eyes. Again, take a deep breath in and begin to energetically feel your environment. Rub your hands together until they tingle. Sit taking deep breaths in and focus on your environment. If a breeze whips across your face, determine whether it is from the wind, a boat, a passerby. Deduce what caused the sensation. Peek and see if you were correct. Continue to sit and observe your environment.

ONE

As you continue practicing this exercise, you will become more observant. By being able to perceive your environment with not only your five senses, but also with your sixth through your aura, you will find yourself moving through your environment much more smoothly. For example, where I once struggled due to my lack of peripheral vision, due to my heightened senses, I can move seamlessly through a crowded grocery store, with a cart no less!

It is important to note that the exercises discussed thus far are limited to gathering information through your intuition. To truly become intuitive, you will utilize this instinctual, physical intuition to assist you in making informed decisions. We'll talk about that a little later. For now, let's move on to the next type of intuition.

CHAPTER FOUR
EMOTIONAL INTUITION

"If I can listen to what he tells me, if I can understand how it seems to him, if I can see its personal meaning for him, if I can sense the emotional flavor which it has for him, then I will be releasing forces of change in him."
Carl Rogers

Emotional intuition is the second form of intuition. Using the exercises outlined in physical intuition, you likely found that while observing the elements of your physical environment you began to get impressions and feelings about the individuals and circumstances within that space. For example, perhaps while sitting in the kitchen you smelled cinnamon. That smell made you think of your mother's apple pie. In that instant, you could have sworn she was sitting beside you as you became overwhelmed by love. Or perhaps when you got home from work you noticed your teenage daughter's backpack slumped in the corner and felt despair, causing you to believe she had a rough day. Impressions or feelings received regarding people and situations such as these are emotional intuition.

Emotional intuition, also known as empathy and emotional intelligence, is an awareness about the current

ONE

state of yourself, someone else or a situation. This awareness is gained through observations, deductions or feelings. The deductions made could be regarding the individual or situations, mood, health, personality or lifestyle. It's important to note that you don't have to be familiar with the person or situation to form opinions.

To better understand emotional intuition, let's look at another couple of examples where emotional intuition is being utilized.

It's 7:30 pm and a shrillness has crept into my daughter's voice. I then observe her aimlessly running in circles with a dazed look. Red circles have formed around her eyes. From experience and mother's instinct, I am certain that even though it is before her bedtime she is ready to go in for the night. That's one example. Another is impressions you have as you approach a friend in a coffee shop. From across the room you notice her hair is up and somewhat frazzled. Not only that, she is fidgeting in her seat. An unease seems to drip off her. Your intuition leads you to believe something is up, has her stressed and the quick coffee date may end up being longer than expected.

Impressions like these are experienced every day from your interactions with family, friends, co-workers, even strangers. These impressions provide useful information about the world around us. The next step of is utilizing those observations to create informed opinions and actions is beneficial. How? We all have our own unique perspectives. These perspectives, the lens through which we view the world, shape the manner in which we approach individuals and situations. Unfortunately, just as when an individual needs glasses, the lens we view the world with is not one size fits all. Not everyone you interact with will see the world through the same lens as you. If that lens is vastly different, it can lead to conflict.

Don't believe me? Take the glasses metaphor. Have you ever ordered glasses and gotten the wrong prescription? Or put on glasses with a prescription vastly different than your own? If you have, you know how uncomfortable or, worse-case scenario, violently ill you can become. The same can be said if you approach an individual using your perspective and it doesn't fit their needs; it can elicit an uncomfortable or even a violent response.

Emotional intuition helps you avoid uncomfortable situations. Because let's be honest: it is rare for an individual to purposefully put another at unease. Rather, discomfort is usually a result of ignorance. By being observant of an individual or situation's current state, you will have more insight and are less likely to be ignorant. And fortunately, doing this doesn't take long. This insight can be gathered in an instant, a minute or over extended lengths of time. Once you've become the observer, you not only have more information and a better understanding of why a circumstance may be the way it is but also how to better relate and respond to it. It assists you in speaking the language of your peers. By doing that, you will have more productive and enjoyable interactions. Without strong emotional intuition, you are unaware of how your actions and words are affecting those around you. As a result, you will likely have unpleasant interactions and may be viewed as naïve, gullible, righteous or tyrannical.

An example of this is an interaction I had with a woman named Mikayla. The two of us had been good friends, but as often happens, life caused us to grow in separate directions. Ultimately the friendship imploded and became irreparable. Why? Because neither of us saw the situation from the other's perspective. She did not see how her actions were negatively impacting me and I did not see how my actions were hurting her. I only learned of her feelings after receiving a letter more than a year later. Perhaps had I used my intuition, the relationship could have been salvaged.

You may be thinking that tapping into your emotional intuition sounds hard. It isn't. Like physical intuition, it is hardwired in each of us. To observe emotional intelligence, one must only watch the interactions of children to see how ingrained empathy is. Children exhibit a kindness and compassion towards others many adults lack. Not only that, they are experts at reading emotions and situations.

My daughter is a perfect example. The day my husband's grandmother passed, despite his efforts to trudge through, she perceived his sadness. At just eighteen months of age, she had little basis upon which to comprehend the emotions he was emitting. Yet, she knew something was wrong and made strides to cheer him up. This included giving him hugs and kisses; bringing him her favorite toy; and when that didn't work, she encouraged him to dance with her. Her actions indicate she observed his sadness, which caused her empathy to kick in, resulting in her efforts to cheer him up.

Her actions demonstrate the hardwired nature of emotional intuition. She had little experience upon which to comprehend the circumstances. My husband wasn't in tears. He wasn't yelling or talking harshly. Since we would be going out of town for the funeral, he was focused on completing projects he had on his plate before we left. My husband didn't exhibit behaviors that were drastically different from a normal day. Yet she knew he was emotionally off and responded to the subtle cues. Human nature kicked in and she wanted to help.

You are not much different. You likely feel the emotional cues and most likely want to help. Unlike my daughter, you, as an adult, however, are more likely to ignore the cues. Think about it for a moment. How often do you know a friend is aggravated or a family member is lonely, but rather than ask them about their feelings, you smile and pretend you don't notice? If you are like me, you may be ashamed to say you do. We all do.

This may lead you to question, "If it is hardwired into us to respond to emotional situations, why do we ignore those feelings"? It is quite simple. As a society, we've been taught to mind our own business. Not to be nosy. And we are told, if individuals want to talk about a situation, they will. Unfortunately, we all know that isn't always the case. Yet, we as adults follow this guidance and let it lead our interactions. Young children, however, have not been societally programed with this concept. That is why they are more attuned to others' feelings and are driven to help one another. Which is better?

There isn't an answer, but it is important to remember there is a reason empathy is hardwired. Humans are social creatures. We are wired, physically and emotionally, for friendship and love. Before being on top of the food chain, those relationships were also necessary for safety. The bigger the group, the higher chance the individual had for long term survival. As such, interpersonal interactions are not only desired but necessary for both our physical and mental well-being.[6]

The positive interactions we get from a supportive, empathetic community continue to be important. Unfortunately, in the westernized world, the need for a supportive community has not changed, but the way we seek it out has. In the 1950s and 1960s, community was found in social institutions such as Rotary Clubs,

ONE

American Legions, church groups and PTAs. Today, community is found online through platforms like Facebook, Instagram and Snapchat. In-person social groups are becoming rarer and rare. In fact, some people avoid and even fear face-to-face social interactions.

The fear or avoidance of social situations occurs for many reasons. The first is fear of our fellow man. In the last chapter, we discussed how in the industrialized world humans have risen to the top of the food chain and have no natural enemies. That's not exactly true. Our fellow humans are natural predators. They can hurt us. And they do.

Our fellow man can inflict physical pain upon us. It may be deliberate, such as being punched in the face in a bar fight. Or it could be unintentional, such as a motor vehicle accident in which someone wasn't paying close enough attention to the road. Either way it happens.

You may be thinking that these situations are few and far between and wouldn't be a reason to avoid a social situation. You might even be thinking that if you're careful, you can avoid these situations. And you may. And the fear of physical harm may not inhibit you.

What is a more likely cause for people avoiding social situations is fear of emotional hurt. Unlike physical harm, emotional harm is inevitable. Someone, at some time, is going to hurt your feelings. In fact, it may happen every day. You might feel snubbed by your work colleagues for going out to lunch and not inviting you. You might feel disrespected by a family member for a comment they make under their breath about you. Or you may hear the people behind you at the checkout line in the grocery store talking unkindly about someone and assume they are referencing you. Situations like these can, and do, cause hurt. It is going to happen.

Hurt is something we want to avoid. Knowing the chances of hurt increases as the number of social interactions increases, causes some to steer clear of in-person social situations. By not participating, individuals can protect themselves from being vulnerable.

Individuals also feel vulnerable and may avoid in-person social situations because they feel awkward and are uncomfortable in their own skin. We live in a society where online we can be anybody we want to be. Think for a moment of someone you know online whose profile picture doesn't match what they look like in person. I have a friend, Karen, whose profile picture is from ten years ago. She was twenty pounds lighter and her blonde hair is now red. We all can think of someone like that; perhaps you are one of them. If that is you, you likely feel uncomfortable meeting with people. The longer you avoid those in-person meetings, the more awkward it becomes. Social graces do take practice, which means you are more likely to avoid the situation in the future. Fortunately, social graces and emotional intuition are ingrained within us all. By strengthening and utilizing these skills, the more comfortable and happier you will become.

Don't believe me? Let me share a sentiment that Bret, a relationship counselor once shared with me. From his extensive experience, he found that if an individual had positive social interactions with a friend, family or colleague, no matter what else is occurring in that relationship, life would be good. The work friend could fire you, but if you have a positive opinion of that colleague, while you may struggle with the concept of finding a new job, you will understand and will have the strength to persevere. On the other hand, if your personal relationships are inadequate, you will suffer no matter how good or bad the situation. For example, if the relationship with the work colleague is insufficient, he could offer you a promotion and you may be skeptical of the promotion with thoughts such as, "Is he trying to get rid of me?" No matter the situation, it will be met with skepticism and distrust.

For this reason, positive relationships are important. What, then, makes a relationship less than adequate? In all circumstances, one and possibly both parties have unmet needs. You may, if you are like many, be tempted to focus on your unmet needs. Unfortunately, you can't change another's behaviors to ensure your needs are being met. You can, however, change or modify your behaviors. That's where emotional intuition comes in. As mentioned, you both likely have unmet needs. The behaviors you wish your loved one would change are likely a result of those unmet needs. By enhancing emotional intuition, you will become better adept at noticing and understanding what those unmet needs are. With that knowledge, you are now equipped to address your loved one's unmet needs, which in turn, will likely result in your own needs being fulfilled.

This skill is what made Millie exemplary at her job and an outstanding community leader. She put the community and her partner's needs first. She did this by listening to the community with her ears and her heart. By doing that she heard and understood her partner's needs. As a result, her needs were met as well. Similarly, you will find that as you address your peers' needs your own needs will be satisfied.

This concept is what Wiccans refer you to the Law of Three. This belief states: what you put out into the world, positive or negative, is returned to you threefold. Experience has proven this tenet to have some merit. Think for a moment. Have you found that when you help a neighbor or friend they turn around and do something nice for you? Sociologists refer to this as the Law of Reciprocity. Simply put, people have the desire to help those who help them. It is a phenomenon that occurs in all cultures.

An example of this theory in action is my husband. One winter he took to snow blowing not only our sidewalk but removing snow for several houses on the block. He did it not for recognition but because it was the neighborly thing to do. That summer we found two gift certificates and a gift for our daughter in our door with thank you notes. Simple acts of kindness lead to strong social connections.

As demonstrated, this can be seen with neighbors and strangers, but it also occurs with family and friends. When you pay attention to your loved ones' needs and go out of your way to help them, they will in turn support you.

Does this sound good to you? If so, let's start exercising your emotional intuition and the law of reciprocity. First, consider that you were given one mouth and two ears for a reason. To honor this concept, try speaking less and listening more. And when you listen, be like Millie and really listen. Don't listen to respond. Don't cast judgment or become offended because the viewpoint being expressed doesn't align with your own. Listen to understand what the person is saying and why they have the opinion they do. If you don't understand the viewpoint or where they are coming from, ask questions until you do! Honor their perspective and be mindful not to insert your own wants and needs until they have had time to express theirs. Put them first.

In addition to listening and asking questions, observe the individual's body language and pay attention to the inflections in their voice. People reveal a lot through their body language, speech patterns and tone of their voice. By fully observing and attuning yourself to these subtle nuances, you will be able to decipher the subtleties of what your peer is saying. Perhaps he or she speaks more passionately about one topic over another. Or perhaps, you observe arms crossed and a downward look while discussing another topic. These nuances can further inform your actions and promote positive interactions in the future.

Want to practice this? Let's look at the following exercise.

Exercise 3
Emotional Intuition Through Listening

To complete this exercise, you will need a partner. Invite a family member, friend, acquaintance or colleague out for coffee. When you meet them, ask them how they are. Then listen. Let them talk. Pretend you are a journalist. Only interrupt to ask questions or add supporting commentary such as, "That sounds challenging" or "You had such strength". Don't stop asking questions until you know the wheres, whats, whens, hows and, most importantly, the whys.

In addition to asking questions, pay attention to their body language. What movements are they making? What is their posture? Do they seem open or closed? Does it change as the conversation continues? After paying attention to their body language, close your eyes and pay attention to how the tone of their voice makes you feel. What emotions do you feel?

> Pay attention to their energy. The conversation may change topics throughout, but it should last no less than an hour. Repeat this exercise at least five times. What did you learn?

What might you learn from this? How might it be applied? Let's explore the following example.

After a long day of consultations, it is not uncommon for me to come home, pour a glass of wine and want to disconnect from the world. I relish my personal space as it is my time to unwind, release the connections I have created throughout the day and recharge my battery. Conversely, at the end of the day my husband wants to talk about the latest news, our business or household chores and projects. We each have different needs and desires. When not perceived or honored, the interactions go very badly. Yearning for conversation, he will try desperately to engage me. I, wanting nothing but quiet and solitude, become annoyed and shut down further. In these moments, we judge and create unfair opinions of the other. I view him as clingy and he views me as detached.

In a situation like this, neither of us is utilizing our emotional intuition. He doesn't know that in a day I may have four clients who lost their loved ones tragically and am trying to release the heartache that was felt by these readings. And I may not know that other than our daughter, he has had no human interaction. We don't know because we didn't take the time to ask or observe. Had either of us asked, it would be more likely that we would both have gotten what we wanted and needed. Had he commented on the fact that I seemed detached, he might have found out about the stressful, heavy day I had. Discussing my heartache might have facilitated my need to detach myself from the pain and satisfied his need for communication. Had I commented on his chattiness, perhaps I would have learned he was feeling lonely and we could have set up a date night giving me the quiet now but promising him that interaction for a later time. We would have understood the underlying needs and addressed them, leaving us both happier.

In addition to listening with your eyes and ears, when using your emotional intuition try to also listen with your heart. Be sympathetic and compassionate. The ability to do this is easy. Think about how you feel when an SPCA commercial comes on and you see those big puppy eyes looking back at you. Or when you are watching the news and you see a mother clutching her baby. In both instances your heartstrings are yanked and you feel the struggle or happiness the individuals on the television are feeling.

If a television, an inanimate device, can elicit those feelings, people in your presence emitting their own vibrations certainly can. In fact, you most likely have experienced this numerous times. An individual may have shared with you the news of the tragic passing of a loved one. The individual may have stayed completely composed, sharing the news without shedding a tear. Despite the outside composure, you may have felt the emotions sloshing around and tugging at his or her insides, causing you to cry when that person had not. Or perhaps while spending time with a friend, you notice he or she seems to be smiling from the inside out. You intuit excitement about something, however nothing out of the ordinary is brought up in conversation. Three days later, however, the friend's engagement is announced.

In instances like these we are listening with our hearts in addition to our heads. As children, like my daughter who didn't think, rather just acted to bring joy to my husband, we trust it. As we age, we rely on those heartfelt feelings less and instead rely on the lessons learned through life experiences. Why? For better or worse, in society phrases like "I'll believe it when I see it" and "History has a tendency of repeating itself" are prevalent and dominate our belief system. With these phrases leading the way, we are taught we must prove our assumptions with cold, hard facts. Until we have evidence, we give individuals and situations the benefit of the doubt. "Innocent until proven guilty," after all.

Conversely, once an individual behaves one way, even if it's only once, phrases like "Once a cheater, always a cheater" and "Can't teach an old dog new tricks" flow off people's lips. In situations like this, there is no consideration that the action may have been a mistake or situational; rather, the individual is characterized by that action forevermore.

It's a no-win situation for both the individual and for the intuitive observer. Why? Unfortunately, explicit proof that supports our intuitive feelings is often hard to obtain. There are many reasons. One, people lie. Sometimes they lie outright; sometimes the lie is by omission; and, sometimes people don't even realize they are lying as they are just sharing the world as they see it through their lens. Not only that, people change. Think for a moment, who you are right now is vastly different than you were ten years ago, ten days ago, maybe even ten minutes ago. Life is fluid. Due to both these situations, you may be left with less than sufficient information to support your intuition. If this happens, you are likely going to trust the lie or what used to be.

Let's explore this by taking a look at Michael. Over the years, due to his erratic behavior, his family suspected

ONE

he was using drugs. He was confronted more than once. Each time he became belligerent and offended. Time and time again he insisted he did not use drugs and was not an addict. His family was left with the facts they could validate. They saw Michael drink... a lot. They knew he smoked pot... sometimes. But since Michael's family never saw him smoke pot, no one knew how much marijuana he smoked. These facts could explain some of his odd behavior.

In addition to those facts, his family knew Michael maintained a good job at a highly reputable institution. He was intelligent and dated intelligent women. He had nice belongings. And he had loyal friends. Overall, he seemed to have a good life. Armed with this information and without evidence of drug abuse, despite the family's suspicions, they were left to take Michael at his word.

The family's instincts were screaming something was wrong and he needed help. With his assurance that everything was okay, those gut feelings were ignored. Turns out his family should have listened to their intuition: Michael did need help. He does battle drug addiction. Cocaine is his drug of choice. Until he hit rock bottom, he hid his issue from everyone.

For years, his family doubted their intuition, doubted themselves. Without indisputable evidence the family would likely still be stifling their intuition. And sometimes they do. When he tells a family member he's clean, many take him at his word. Rather than taking his word, they should as "how long?" This question is important because his family has discovered that Michael's definition of being clean is clean right "now". But, he could have used a day or two ago. This is different than what the inquirer's assumption is thinking he'd been clean for a week, a month, or perhaps even longer.

This example demonstrates that to be emotionally intuitive one must not only listen to one's gut feelings but a lot of questions may be needed to validate those feelings. Otherwise, society's philosophies of "Innocent until proven guilty" and "I need to see it with my own eyes" can have a negative impact on one's emotional intuition. Think about Michael for a moment. For years, his family doubted themselves. Imagine how many people came into his life in that time who had the same suspicion, such as people he lost contact with due to his lifestyle. How many of those individuals were told they were wrong? How many never had their suspicions validated? And because of the lack of validation, how many doubt their intuitive feelings today? It is likely that there are many.

Situations like Michael's, where there is an immense amount of circumstantial evidence but no concrete validation, cause us to distrust our intuition. Think about how many times this happens on a daily basis. Multiple that by seven and then by fifty-two. You likely have a pretty big number at this point. Now think about that over a lifetime. No wonder we doubt our intuition. Nevertheless, you can overcome that doubt. How? It goes back to being curious. When you have a suspicion or gut feeling, ask lots of questions. When you get answers, don't just listen with your ears. Listen with your heart. Watch a person's body language and facial expressions. Pay attention to all the clues you are being given, because, as we have established, what an individual tells you through words may be a lie. If you are paying attention to the whole picture, you will discover the truth. A person may be good at telling you what you want to hear, but few people are good liars. Their behavior gives them away. They may not look you in the eye. They may fidget. The story may change. They may be overly excited and it may be apparent they are holding good news back. Pay attention to those behaviors and expressions.

It goes without saying that to listen you are required to talk to people. I know this can be scary, especially, as noted above, as we become more and more immersed in a technological culture where face to face communication is happening less and less. Hiding behind computers and smart phone screens as we opt to communicate through e-mail, text, tweets and snapchats as opposed to in person or over the phone hinders emotional intuition. Electronic communication removes the subtle nuances of body language and tone of voice. Without these cues, we become further detached from our fellow man and their needs, which, as discussed earlier, results in misunderstandings and problems. A silly example of this is an interaction between my husband and myself.

We were texting about dinner. Having gone back and forth, we had it narrowed down to spaghetti or chicken pot pie. He indicated his preference was spaghetti. My simple response "Fine" caused my husband to become irritated. Why? Because he perceived my response to indicate I was displeased with the choice, whereas in saying "Fine," I meant, "Sure, that's ok with me," as I didn't have a preference either way. In that moment, because he didn't hear my voice or see my body language, he had nothing but the words themselves to understand my meaning. And his interpretation of the response, "Fine," was that I was being snarky. This miscommunication caused hurt and frustration that was completely unnecessary. Unfortunately, due to the nature of our society today, this is becoming more and more common. So, if you have the option, face to face communication is best. If you must text or email, be verbose. The more descriptive you are, the less chance there is for misinterpretation.

Another benefit of face to face communication is that it will bolster your emotional intuition. The more interaction you have with individuals while using the tools mentioned above, the greater awareness of the nuances of situations you will obtain. Not only will it allow you to respond in the moment more appropriately, but you will also anticipate future problems and either avert them or lessen the blow.

My husband is an example of this. He likes to help others by fixing problems. This used to cause frequent awkwardness at the holistic center where he and I keep offices. The reason? He has a desire to be of service. This desire caused him to enthusiastically and frequently approach the proprietor with ideas of ways the center could operate more efficiently both administratively and technologically. Unfortunately, overwhelmed with all her current to-dos, she did not want to embark on any additional tasks. As a result, these unsolicited ideas fell upon deaf ears.

That did not stop my husband. He didn't recognize the growing tension between him and her. Nor did he notice she was avoiding him. He didn't recognize it because he wasn't listening with his eyes, ears and heart. He didn't notice the circles under her eyes or the fidgeting she would have while he discussed ideas. Nor did he feel her stress. Rather, he was focused on his need and his desire to be of service. Fortunately, as he spent more time with her, he did notice the subtle signs she was giving him. He paid attention to the pile on her desk. If it seemed larger than normal, he put off discussing his latest idea until she seemed less busy. Also, rather than making his own assumptions on where the center could use improvement, he asked her what she would like to see improved and what wasn't working for her. By doing those simple things, the relationship between the two of them improved. Not only that, as time went on he became better at guessing what processes she would like improved. Most importantly, he found that his needs were being met as he became Mr. Fix-It.

In this situation, my husband used all the tools to strengthen his emotional intuition. First, he used the exercise outlined in physical intuition and became more observant of the physical environment. He noticed the piles of papers on her desk. He noticed the circles under her eyes and how quickly she responded. He paid attention to body language. He also stopped making assumptions about what she needed and asked questions, inquiring what her priorities were. And he listened with his heart and didn't judge. Amazingly, as he changed, so did she. The law of reciprocity does work and energy will move towards a neutral state.

To have the success my husband had in one of your situations, something you are doing will need to shift. If you want to see change, lead by example. Be the person to take the first step towards compromise. Be honest, transparent, speak from the heart and take personal responsibility for your actions. Become the person people admire. If you are being the best person you can be, you will get the same in return. For example, think about the last time you were with a person you admire. Did you find yourself emulating that behavior? Or perhaps sharing more than you intended? Probably.

Be prepared, however. Being honest and speaking from the heart does have some disadvantages. You will be surprised at just how much people are moved to open up to you. A friend of mine once told me, "Dawn, you are like truth serum. I just can't help but share all my deepest held beliefs and fears with you." While part of this may have been that she assumed I already knew, more likely it was because I was transparent with her. Because I was genuine, she knew I wouldn't judge nor would I share.

Practice these simple steps while interacting with your peers and you will find yourself more attuned to who they are as opposed to who you think they are. It's a lot easier than you may think and the payoffs to you are tremendous. Not only will you make *them* feel good, *you* will feel good, even if you don't get what you want because ultimately, you will find you are getting what you need.

ONE

CHAPTER FIVE
SPIRITUAL INTUITION

"Faith is to believe in what you do not see; the reward of faith is to see what you believe."
Saint Augustine

We've talked about physical and emotional intuition. They were easy to describe and provide tips on how to strengthen them because ultimately your environment provides the answers. That means all you have to do is become more observant.

Spiritual intuition, on the other hand, is more difficult to explain. It is less concrete. This form of intuition rarely manifests as something you can see with your eyes, hear with your ears or touch with your hands. Rather, it is a knowing. This knowing is usually quite strong, persistent, and usually lacks rational explanation, which can be frustrating. You'll find yourself knowing but don't know why.

How does spiritual intuition manifest itself? It most commonly occurs when you ask yourself a question and know the answer, even though you have no previous knowledge or background to support the conclusion you've made. For example, suppose I were to observe a bird and ask you, "What type of bird is that?" To your surprise, you respond, "A yellow tanger." Why were you surprised? How is this spiritual intuition? Assume you know little about birds; the bird is not yellow, it's brown; not only that, you have never heard of a yellow tanger, yet you had the answer and were correct. That is spiritual intuition.

This type of intuition, like its physical and emotional counterparts, occurs all the time. Do you notice it? Probably not. The information comes spontaneously, and just as quickly as it pops into your mind it is gone. For example, you are humming a song while you get into the car only to find that song is playing on the radio when the car is turned on. Or when your phone rings, you know who it is. You may even use it, like I do, when you are lost. If I can't get to my phone to connect to GPS, I will pause and ask which way to go: left, right or straight. By following my first instinct, more times than not, I get to exactly where I wanted to be. There is no logical explanation, but it works.

Not having a logical explanation isn't exactly true. It is true we can't see how we accessed the information, nor do we have the tools to demonstrate how it was obtained, but, as the discussion about energy demonstrated, we are all connected. And the information we accessed is out there, somewhere. Logically, since we are all connected and the information is available, doesn't it make sense that we should be able to access it? And we did access it after all. Therefore, a more accurate statement is, we don't currently have the tools to measure or validate the occurrence, but that doesn't mean that someday we won't have them. History has demonstrated that as humans evolve, we are continuously able to measure our environment and explain that which could not be explained in the past. Throughout history, theories that were once far-fetched have been proven valid. For example, there was a time when people believed the world was flat. Despite this popular belief, some scientists proposed the world was round. These men were laughed at for the belief. Turns out, they were right. The world is round. When it comes to intuition, it is likely science just needs time to catch up and demonstrate it is a real occurrence and we aren't all bonkers!

Until science can catch up, however, people like you and me are left to hold onto our beliefs and have faith. For many, that faith comes through spirituality and religion. Most, if not all, religious and spiritual teachings share the belief that a greater universal knowledge exists that connects us all. Further, each belief system is designed to assist an individual's soul evolve. This growth is commonly referred to as enlightenment. A belief in the Kabbalah describes this process beautifully. The belief is that the moment before birth all the mysteries of the universe are whispered into a baby's ear. In that moment, the baby fully understands its purpose. When that new babe takes its first breath, however, that knowledge is forgotten. While the child may not consciously remember, that knowledge continues to reside within. The goal of life is to uncover those truths through unique experiences.

The hidden truths within ourselves form the energy we tap into while utilizing spiritual intuition. All knowledge is available through the energies of spiritual intuition. Led by the greater unconsciousness, God, higher selves or spirit guides, whatever term you want to use, when we tap into those energies we can receive novel information, such as the name of a bird we are unfamiliar with, but we can also obtain insights regarding ourselves that can bring us closer to achieving our desires and our purpose. Anything is possible.

Knowing that anything is possible and that all knowledge is accessible is exciting. It may make you feel like you are part of something greater than yourself. It may also empower you, make you feel special and give you purpose. Ultimately, it should give you hope.

At the same time, knowing that all knowledge is around us but cannot always be accessed can be frustrating. For example, think about all the time you spent mulling over a big decision. Perhaps it was hours, days, months or even years. Think of all that lost time and lost sleep due to that situation. Then think about all the stress you felt over making that decision. A decision that based on this theory likely already had an outcome. It did, but at the same time it didn't. The outcome of that decision was not which path you chose to take. Rather, it was the lessons you learned through the trials and tribulations you had along the way. The lost sleep and stress were worth it.

That doesn't make the reality any less frustrating. Think for a moment how much simpler life would be if we could use this information to our benefit. Take, for example, the days my daughter misplaced her binkie and I found myself frantically searching the house from top to bottom as she cried and whimpered, "inky." The knowledge that the universe knew exactly where that binkie was but wouldn't help in the moment was frustrating. It was as if the universe were taunting me. In a calmer, more rational state of mind, I recognized the universe was not taunting me. It, as stated in a previous chapter, does not choose sides. It does not purposefully withhold information from anyone without purpose. With that in mind, I recognized that there were lessons in the missing binkie. My daughter learned how to calm herself, and I learned how to let her.

ONE

As demonstrated, the frustration experienced had its reason. Although I didn't like it, and you are likely not going to like it either, it is our job to go through struggles, learn lessons and unearth that knowledge through a lifetime of experiences. If we were meant to know everything, we wouldn't be here.

Unfortunately, those lessons and experiences can be uncomfortable, painful and confusing. At times you may have asked, "Why me?" or "What did I do to deserve this?" Or you may have felt the universe is a cruel prankster dangling a carrot over your head to see how high you will jump. Faye is a great example of this. Before the age of fifty, she lost two husbands to cancer. Her son, shortly after his thirtieth birthday was also taken by the nasty disease. She questions, "Why?" And in moments like these it is hard to understand why, let alone have faith. Yet having faith that circumstances are pushing you towards your soul's purpose is important. Bad things do happen to good people, and it's usually for a reason. Unfortunately, understanding those reasons, especially when they don't align with your wants, is hard. This is like a craving you have for a cupcake while dieting. In the moment, you crave that cupcake, but in the grand scheme of things, you want to lose fifty pounds. The struggle not to eat the cupcake is real. It is difficult. You might deny yourself the cupcake. You may find yourself bitter as the thought that one cupcake won't hurt runs through your head. And then as you think about the fifty pounds you want to lose, you may question, "Is it worth it?" That internal debate between desire and goal is life. You have desires and want instant gratification. You also want to avoid pain, but just like the diet, which requires pain from exercise, change in diet, etc., life will be painful. Are you going to push through it?

Pushing through it is where faith comes in, because unlike in the diet, where you know you want to lose fifty pounds, if you believe the words of the Kabbalah, you don't know what you are shooting for. This makes it hard to understand how those times of pain are making you stronger and furthering your goals. Unfortunately, you can't know the outcome. If you did, you wouldn't have the same experiences and lessons learned. For example, think to a time when someone spilled the beans about a surprise someone else was planning for you. When the surprise ultimately came, it probably lacked luster. The same thing is true when it comes to finding that knowledge deep within you. Instead of being stressed, have faith that you are exactly where you are meant to be.

Why is having faith so important? Because the more you try to force your mission, the farther you get from it. The reason for this is simple and goes back to what was stated before: you do not know what your true purpose is. You may think you do. And you very well might be on the right path, but you will only ever scratch the surface of knowing your true purpose. Anything else falls into the category of your wants. The more you work towards it, the more committed you become, the further you get from the soul's truth. Faith will bring you back because spiritual intuition is innate.

As with physical and emotional intuition, again you only have to turn to small children to observe spiritual intuition at play and how you can tap into your own spiritual intuition. Children are blank slates. They do not have any preconceptions or notions. As a result, they are more aware of the spiritual influences around them. Those spiritual influences are stronger around children because they exist in both the spiritual realm and the physical one of earth. This is the natural order of the world and our natural state. The child's existence in both worlds is demonstrated by the presence of imaginary friends and monsters under the bed. Yes, they really do exist. If you doubt it, ask a child to describe these "friends." A woman I know, Cara did this. To her shock, her daughter described her father and brother in vivid detail. Are you thinking Cara's daughter may have seen pictures and the descriptions are simply a result of a little girl's imagination? If you are, you'd be wrong. Not only did Cara's daughter describe their appearance, she also commented on their personality and made seemingly random comments about the individuals. Those "random" comments were identifiers of the two spirits that Cara had all but forgotten. Not only that, she was certain she had never mentioned these facts to her daughter. This happens more often than not. Ask a child in your life, and you will likely receive similar feedback.

This connection to both worlds is fleeting, not because children lose the ability, but because they are conditioned to recognize the difference between "reality," that which exists on the earthly plane (the one adults have been conditioned to see), and "make believe," that which exists on the spiritual plane and is less tangible. Children are taught, if they can't touch it, it isn't real. Just as in the story of Peter Pan, where children as they age can no longer see fairies, those imaginary friends and monsters disappear. With them, some of that knowledge slips away and becomes more difficult to access.

As they age, children depend on their intuition less and less as they are taught to depend upon reasoning and logic. They look for facts to support their hypotheses, for without the evidence it is simply a guess. And their intuition begins to collect dust, but like a library, that information is still there. It sits, waiting to be called upon.

And even though we might not do it knowingly, every single one of us peeks into that vault of knowledge from time to time. Individuals do it for silly things, such as while gambling at a casino and selecting a "lucky" machine that lo-and-behold, pays off. Or they do it to get a "vibe" off of someone, checking in if they are on the up and up or not. However, the most common way individuals tap into that knowledge occurs when they pray.

Prayer is a form of meditation. It is a time during which an individual quiets the mind. In prayer, individuals often ask for insight. With quieted thoughts and focused intent, they send their hopes to the universe and ask for understanding. Prayer serves as a private conversation with the universe. As with physical and emotional intuition, in which you are not confined to only receiving the information as a passive participant, you can also become an active participant and interact with the world.

With that in mind, when was the last time you prayed? If it is not something you make a habit of, chances are it was during a time you were struggling. Individuals often turn to God, angels, deceased loved ones, the universe, the source, whatever you call it, in times of heartache and grief. In these times of hardship, individuals seek an explanation for why the bad circumstance occurred, perhaps even asking, "What did I do wrong?" Individuals ask these questions because we are trained to believe everything happens for a reason. When logical reasoning doesn't offer a solution, even non-believers go outside themselves, out of their realm of understanding to discover "Why?"

As you likely know from reflecting on the last time you prayed, the moment you surrender yourself to the universe is rarely the moment you are met with insights and wisdom you seek. Without the sought-after answers, some walk away defeated, still looking for answers. Many more walk away with peace and resolve to move forward. For while answers were not found, they found love, support and healing. With this new resolve, over time, the wisdom comes.

To facilitate that wisdom and strengthen your spiritual intuition, practice prayer and meditation. If you are not familiar with prayer, here is an exercise you can use to deepen your connection.

Exercise 4
Prayer

The first step is to choose one item, only one, for which you desire insight or resolution. Be specific. Don't use a broad topic, for example family. If you are interested in family, choose one family member. Got your topic?

Now, find a comfortable, quiet space where you will not be interrupted. Dim the lights as it minimizes outside stimulation. In prayer, it is important that you go within. Get into a comfortable position and take three deep breaths in and out. Allow that breath to fill your lungs. As you are breathing, take time to quiet your mind. By quieting you mind, you open yourself to receiving insight.

Once your mind has quieted, focus on the selected topic. Talk, out loud or in your head, about the topic. Voice your concerns. Voice your desires. Voice the strengths of the situation. The weaknesses. The pros. The cons. Talk through the situation. If you are a visual person, play the scenarios out in your mind. Think about it until you

> cannot think about it anymore. More importantly, think and talk about it until you have a resolution or conclusion.
>
> Then the hard part. Sit in quiet. Stay put for at least five minutes, longer is better. Set a timer if you struggle. Pay attention to your breath. Pay attention to your feelings. Repeat this exercise on a regular basis.

As you practice this exercise, you may find you don't receive clear answers and signs. You may not see, hear or taste. Don't expect to. Those answers don't come immediately. They take time, patience and effort. Rather, you will find yourself being filled with feelings and hunches. Trust these hunches and walk away from each prayer with conviction and hope. With hope and an open-mind, these feelings will manifest into signs that appear in your day to day interactions. These signs come in the form of your desires, the words and actions of others, and the way in which the universe aligns in your favor. For example, when I prayed for insight regarding my daughter's schooling, the next day I ran into a friend who raved about the preschool my husband and I were considering sending our daughter to. The universe aligned. The more this happens, you will find your faith growing. Before you know it, that faith will run deep through your veins and your spiritual intuition will flow like breath. It will be gentle and invigorating. It will be something you don't have to think about doing as it will be habit. Additionally, it will become something you can't and don't want to live without.

ONE

SECTION TWO
GETTING THE MESSAGES

ONE

CHAPTER SIX
WHAT HAPPENS WHEN YOU USE YOUR INTUITION

"The more you trust your intuition, the more empowered, stronger, and happier you become."
Giselle Bundchen

Physical, emotional and spiritual intuition are so intertwined it is difficult to use any of the three individually or in isolation from the others. Nor should you want to. When not used together, you can't fully grasp a situation. If decisions are based on information limited to one form of intuition, there will be disruption to your life. For example, an individual wishing to be led solely by spiritual intuition is likely to be ungrounded, make impractical decisions and might even become righteous. Why? Because spiritual intuition is focused on life's ultimate purpose without a care in the world for your physical existence. When focused on spirituality, you may not worry about having a roof over your head or food in your belly because that's physical intuition's job. Nor would you worry about your emotional happiness or the stress lack of security could cause. Spiritual intuition's focus is solely to assist you in achieving your life purpose.

ONE

An example of this is a woman named Tessa. She felt guided to write a book as she felt it was her life purpose to inspire people. Admirably, Tessa wrote the book. Once it was completed, she immediately quit her job with the intention of taking on speaking engagements and promoting her masterpiece. Fast track to a year later. Because Tessa hadn't created a plan for how to distribute her book or put money aside to cover her expenses while she gained momentum, she was struggling to pay her bills. On top of that, the stress of not having enough to pay her bills and disappointment over slow success caused a flare up of a chronic condition. Had she relied on all her intuitions might the outcome have been different? Perhaps. We won't know.

Similarly, just as much harm can be done by only paying attention to your emotional intuition. Individuals whose empathy drives them often find themselves continuously doing for others and not taking their own emotional needs into account. They want others to be happy above their own happiness. Like the individual who focuses on spiritual intuition, they fail to consider their physical needs. They also forget to consider their life purpose.

Caroline is a perfect example of this. As the mother of five children and two grandchildren, her family always comes first. She wishes for nothing more than their safety and happiness. Wishing to assist her children in any way she can, she often neglects her own physical needs. She has, on more than one occasion, lent her kids her car only to leave herself without transportation. She has also neglected her own spiritual desires. She yearns to connect with the universe and receive messages from her angels, but she often finds herself showing up late or not being able to attend a class at all due to her children's schedules and her inability to say no. While this example is not as devastating as Tessa's, because of Caroline's empathy, she finds her physical and spiritual intuition thwarted and she finds herself wanting more.

Finally, if you were to only pay attention to the physical energies, while you would likely be successful, without empathy and spiritual direction, you might find the success to be empty and lonely. Without empathy, individuals find themselves hurting people along the way, whereas without spiritual insight, they find themselves without purpose. Without purpose, sooner or later they are likely to lose the success they worked so hard to achieve. Success is temporary. Love, friendships and legacies are forever. As these individuals tend to lead more solitary existences, examples are harder to come by. However, I do have one.

Rose started a business with her friend, Melissa. They were in the right place at the right time and served a niche population. Over the course of only a couple years, their business more than doubled in size. As it grew, Rose became confident and cocky in her savviness. She became obsessed with making more money, even if it strayed from the original goal. Due to this and her ego, her partner and many other individuals stepped aside. She lost friends and her emotional support system, but she had money. The question is, however, for how long? Her clients have expressed she is less attentive to their needs and that the quality of the product she sells has diminished. As a result, many of her clients have started to go to other sources for their service. By not paying attention to her spiritual calling and being driven by success, her vision for the future is being clouded. Will she be happy in the long haul? Time will tell. Would you be?

In each example, it is apparent that by focusing on one intuition over another, failure and dissatisfaction are inevitable. For these reasons, it is important for individuals to seek balance in their lives. Only by striking a balance among your physical, emotional and spiritual needs will you find peace and joy. Utilizing all forms of intuition can help you do this. It is also important to note that there will be times in your life when one need and intuition, be it physical, emotional or spiritual, is dominant. For example, if you have the flu, your physical needs and intuition will be dominant. Or, if you have just had a baby, it is likely your emotional needs and intuition will be central. Overall, you will find they are evenly distributed, but if you find yourself paddling in circles, evaluate what is driving you, as your intuitions may be out of balance and need readjustment.

Finding that balance and listening to your intuition is easy, yet the persistence it takes is hard. You must be observant. You must pray. You must have faith. You mustn't give up. Once you start doing these things, you will find you perceive the subtle nudges that are all around you. The universe does provide. Once you begin pursuing balance and actively listening, life becomes "easy" or as my grandmother would say, "you are blessed with luck."

I laugh when I use the term "easy" or "luck." Why? Because to be quite honest, it doesn't always feel that way. You will find that even when life is easy, it is still work. You won't find yourself at home eating bon-bons all day. Not sure what I mean?

Let's compare life and the utilization of intuition to kayaking on a river. When not using your intuition, you have in your mind the direction in which you would like to go. You aren't paying attention to the way the current is flowing, nor are you paying attention to the winds and dark clouds on the distant horizon. As a result, at times you are moving with the current. Other times you are not. During the times your destination aligns with the current (your life's purpose), you don't use a lot of effort. The current takes you where you want to go and does the work. In those moments, all you need to do is steer the boat and the ride is easy. On the other hand, when your destination is against the current, not only do you have to steer, but you must work hard to go even an inch. Even if you try your hardest, all that effort does not guarantee you will arrive at your intended destination, for depending on the strength of the current you may still find yourself being pulled with the tow, not to mention the clouds in the distance. Those dark and stormy clouds may catch up to you. Without awareness of them, you may find yourself unprepared in the middle of a storm.

    An example of an individual going against the tide is my husband. Shortly after we were married, he lost his job – not ideal but not devastating as he was unhappy in the position. Additionally, as an independent IT consultant he already had several steady clients. Ultimately, the budget was impacted, but it was his ego that took the bigger hit.

    The ego continued to suffer as he applied to job after job and heard very little back. After being out of a traditional job for almost a year, an opportunity to sign on as an independent agent with a sales company presented itself. We knew the business worked since friends made their income from it. I had hesitations as the job didn't seem to suit his skill set. He agreed but was eager to take the opportunity. After joining the company, my husband worked hard at the business. He followed the business

ONE

plan and utilized every tactic recommended. He listened to podcast after podcast, attended all training seminars, and joined work groups to learn strategies that worked for other agents. Unfortunately, the harder he worked the less impact it seemed to have. Finally, after exhausting all strategies, he walked away. When he did, a weight was lifted and something surprising happened. Suddenly individuals seeking an independent IT consultant approached him and his consulting business blossomed. He had been fighting the current all along and once his energies were open to receiving, the universe provided.

Fighting against the current and following what seems best occurs more often than one would expect. This causes many people to struggle, whereas when you use your intuition and allow yourself to go with the flow (pardon the pun) you don't have to work as hard. At this point you may be saying, "How do I go with the flow?"

The first step to ensure you are not fighting against the current is to evaluate how a given circumstance is making you feel. If you are feeling turmoil, despair, hopelessness, agony or something along those lines, you need to pause and reflect. In that moment of reflection, remember that going with the current doesn't guarantee the ride will be smooth. In life, much like a river, you can't control the flow or the twists and turns it will take. Your journey may take you through rapids or even a waterfall. And during those times, the journey may be scary and unpredictable. In the circumstance you are thinking about, is the discomfort and fear you are facing a result of the difficult journey? Is it a growing pain? Or is the discomfort a continual symptom of the situation? Does the situation change?

How can you tell? Check in. Is the situation, as in a river with rapids and waterfalls, short lived? While harrowing in the moment, once you have passed those obstacles they are often followed by calm waters. Is there the potential for calmer waters in the distance? If you are not sure, the easiest way to determine if calmer waters are in your future is to again pause and reflect. Objectively observe the situation around you. This is a time to use all three forms of intuition to ensure balance in your life. Be sure to check in to see if your physical goals, be they financial, health, career, or educational, are being met. If not, do you have knowledge of this, or is it likely that this will change? Then check in the with your emotional goals. Are you happy? Is the current situation impacting your relationships positively? Negatively? Is the status likely to change? After checking in with your physical and emotional self, check in with the spiritual self. Are you following your dreams? Is the current circumstance moving you closer to accomplishing your dreams? Can you see yourself doing what you are doing in twenty years? After asking these, and any other questions you may have, if you find yourself being pulled in any one direction, pay attention to it.

 Let's explore an example of an individual who has utilized this process and is following the tides of her intuition. Elle is a talented artist and craftsman. She has run a successful business for many years. She teaches locally, nationwide and at international conferences. Her art shows are always well attended, and her art is known for eliciting everything from tears to roaring laughter. Over the last few years, she has been pulled in another direction. Following her intuition, Elle has started to explore this new direction and has received great feedback. The initial dabbling wasn't enough, however. Her heart and intuition have led her to believe she is supposed to jump head first into this new endeavor and leave the art behind.

The prospect of this, while exciting, is also terrifying. While making her decision as to what road to take, Elle first checked in with her physical self. Art is her primary income stream. As a business owner, she has already committed herself to several business expenses, the biggest being her leased studio space and the utility bills that accompany that. In support of this new venture, Elle already has satisfied clients. These individuals are influential and have offered to assist her in growing her clientele. After checking in with her physical self, she determined she would be okay moving forward with the uncertainties, so, she moved on to evaluate how her emotional body felt.

Elle loves creating art. She loves seeing the looks on people's faces when they are moved by one of her pieces, but she realized she provokes the same emotions through this new endeavor she is giddy about. And, just because she isn't making a business out of art, doesn't mean she can't still create. Ultimately, she determined her emotional self was okay with moving forward with the new endeavor.

Finally, she checked in with her spiritual self. When Elle got here, there was no question; she knew she was supposed to dive in. After making that determination and finding peace with her decision, she dove in by restructuring her website to feature her latest endeavor and removed all memories of her art. Upon doing this, the tides moved her in the direction and the universe provided. Not only did she find the work she was doing easier and more enjoyable, but her phone rang with four new clients. The universe *does* provide.

Elle was fortunate. Her transition was smooth. And it was relatively quick. That isn't always the case. Life is

WHAT HAPPENS WHEN YOU USE YOUR INTUITION

not always predictable or steady. Change can happen fast, or it can happen slowly. And like a river, it can be erratic. Think about a waterfall. At the top, the water moves fast and is strong. While crashing down, there is no current because the water is in freefall. But once you hit the bottom, the water is smooth and calm. It changes quickly.

These changes, these forces, will happen whether you are going with or fighting against the current. What then, is the benefit of going with the current? If you have been going with the current, you haven't used all your energy. You let the current do the work. Therefore, you have the energy to move through rough water, whereas, if you have been fighting the current, you may be tired and less equipped to deal with the circumstances as they arise. Either way, when the path in life becomes rough, you are going to move forward. It's a matter of how mentally, emotionally and physically prepared you are for the journey.

It is important to note that at any time during the journey of life you can choose to go with the flow. When you do, you will find yourself becoming observant and using your intuition. And before long, you will find yourself becoming a seasoned seaman, adept at reading the currents (picking up the signs) and navigating the waters. You will pay attention to the size of the waves, the speed of the current, the depth of the water, the landscape of the shore as well as the length of the horizon. All of these are indicators of what the river ahead will bring. You will use all forms of intuition. This knowledge allows you to prepare for what will come. Prepared when you reach rocky waters, you will be better able to navigate them, meaning you and your ship come out less worn.

Whether you know it or not, you are likely already good at using your intuition. Chances are you use it every

ONE

day at work. For example, a successful stockbroker reads the trends of the market and has a sense which direction investors are going to sway. A compassionate counselor is going to be skilled at using intuition to read a client's emotional state to assist in healing the client's heartaches. A nurse is likely going to be able to know a patient's level of pain before it is shared with him or her. Think for a moment: how do you use your intuition at work to navigate the challenges you face?

You probably realized when thinking about the previous question, intuition assists you in doing your job well. It was probably one of the first on-the-job skills you obtained. It is the routine you fall into and the cellular memory that kicks in when faced with an obstacle. If you think about it, when faced with obstacles at work you rarely have a great deal of time to think over what is the best option. Let's take, for example, a teacher who witnesses two children getting into a fight. The teacher doesn't pause to determine who is right, who is wrong, or weigh all the pros and cons of how to best handle the situation. Rather, intuition assists in making decisions. In your job, you have probably experienced the same thing.

Making decisions and using your intuition in your job is easy. Why? One, because in many jobs you have become programmed on how to behave. Experience supports your decisions. Additionally, individuals tend to be less emotionally invested in their jobs. As a result, they tend to focus more on their spiritual and physical intuitions.

As you grow your intuition, you can expand the intuitive skills you use at work into all areas of your life, which is especially important when making decisions. At these forks in the road, you have the choice of the hard and fast route, the slow and leisurely one, or you may even choose to go off-road for an adventure. Just like at work, you rarely have much time to think about which way you'd like to go. And chances are, if you wait too long, the current is going to sweep you in one direction or another. Indecision is a decision after all. When you choose not to make decisions, you are letting the universe decide. In doing this, the universe will guide you in the manner it sees fit, which means you may not like the path that has been chosen for you. The universe, after all, is focused on your spiritual evolution and doesn't weigh your emotional or physical needs as heavily. As a result, the road may be a little bumpier. The more you use your intuition to assist in making decisions, the easier it will become to get to your destination.

Let's explore an example. Before my husband and I wed, the question on everyone's mind was, "Are you going take his last name?" It is after all the traditional thing to do. And, while he didn't say it, he wanted me to, but I loved my last name. It was my identity. I struggled with giving that up, especially since I didn't care for his last name. It suited him, not me. I dragged my feet. As the big day neared, the urgency to decide set in, but I still couldn't find it within me to choose what we would be announced as or what I would be called. Finally, I accepted that a decision needed to be made. I checked in with my physical intuition, which indicated having the same last name would create stability and harmony within the marriage. My emotional intuition was torn. I wanted to make my soon-to-be husband happy, but I couldn't shake that his last name didn't feel right. And spiritually, everything told me no.

So where did that leave me? What did I do? I turned to the universe and asked that it give me a sign. The next day my then fiancé came to me with an odd and

ONE

endearing proposal. He suggested we take his middle name as our last name. It was a suitable last name since it had originally been a family surname. During his pitch that we take his middle name, he professed that by taking a new last name together we would be creating a unique identity for our new family. At that point, all my intuitions approved. The universe had helped. I went with the current and I was put exactly where I ultimately knew I was supposed to be. The universe has a funny way of doing that.

As demonstrated in this example, the decision is ultimately yours to make. The universe through your intuition acts like a kind parent. It is always there whenever you need it. And it won't tell you what to do; rather, it will guide you towards the decision that will bring you not only short term but also long term happiness. It always offers guidance and usually alternative solutions. All you have to do is ask.

Asking is hard, especially at first when you will feel as if you are talking but no one is listening. The more you ask, the easier it becomes. You will receive and understand the guidance provided. Once it starts coming, be prepared for repetition. You will get the same message over and over and over again. This will be annoying. You might also start to believe that you are missing something. You aren't.

The universe repeats itself. Why? We are dense. We don't get the message the first time. If we do, we don't trust it. My friend Justin is a great example of this. Justin asks for signs and messages all the time. I laugh when I see him playing with the Tarot. He will ask a question and pull a card. When he gets the answer, he quizzically will state, "Really?" and immediately pull another. The second card, as well as the third and fourth, all give him the same answer, yet he needs the repetition and until that fourth card doesn't believe it. That's with signs right in front of his face, but what about the unsolicited signs? He might need ten or twenty. That's why the universe repeats.

The universe also repeats because in life we find ourselves facing the same set of circumstances and decisions time and time again. There are several reasons for this. The first and obvious one is that you did not learn the lesson the first time around. Possibly, but what is more likely is that the situation, while similar, has new complexities. The new angles allow your soul to grow. Each time you are faced with a situation, you become better at it.

Let's explore the concept with this example. My friend Emily and I would schedule coffee dates. Unfortunately, nine times out of ten she would cancel. It didn't matter when it was. During the week, weekends, daytime, nighttime, even spontaneous get togethers would be thwarted. At first this was disappointing, but then it became downright aggravating. She would insist on us getting together, which meant because she was "busy," I would rearrange my schedule and the times I would normally book clients I opened up for her, only to have her to turn around and stiff me. This was literally taking money of my pocket. Finally, I let her know she would have to arrange her schedule around when I was free, not the reverse. Since then I have only seen her twice.

I stood my ground. What was more important, I learned my lesson. Shortly after drawing the line in the sand with this friend, I became acquainted with Olivia. When we tried to get together, she exhibited all the same tendencies of the friend I just discussed. My intuition was screaming at me and after being stiffed once, I gently informed her of the value of my time and that if we were to get together, she would need to respect that. And you know what, she did.

The situation repeated itself and my intuition helped me see the signs. In response, I demonstrated I had learned my lesson. The more skilled you are at interpreting the signs, the more obvious these repetitions will become and the better prepared you will be for what is to come. Not only that, it empowers you because you will have chosen the path you are taking rather than being caught up and having the circumstances be decided for you.

CHAPTER SEVEN
FEAR OF INTUITION

"May your choices reflect your hopes not your fears."
Nelson Mandela

At this point it is probably clear that intuition is simply becoming more observant of the world around you. After reading about the benefits of intuition, you may also be excited to know you have the ability to use intuition and to obtain a greater understanding of yourself and the world around you. Despite that, you may find yourself hesitant. While you yearn for that connection, you may be afraid of it. You might even perceive your intuition to be evil or a curse, not a blessing. With all the positive aspects of intuition, why might someone fear it?

While every individual has different fears and reasons for avoiding using their intuition, here are the most common.

It is against the Bible. Well, in some people's opinion.

This is by far the most common objection. From experience, I can tell you that many clients and students upon sitting with me feel the need to proclaim they are reformed Catholics (although I believe this could be expanded to any Christian church). After informing me that they are reformed, they almost always follow the statement with, "If my family knew I was here, they would disown me!" Why do they feel the need to tell me this? They believe, or know someone who believes, that Christianity, the religion they turn to as a moral compass, views intuition as evil. In this statement, they unconsciously or consciously are asking for my assurance that intuition isn't evil or wrong, which I offer. What speaks volumes, however, is that despite this fear, these individuals are still there. Despite their concerns, the need for connection with their loved ones or the universe leaves them searching for something they haven't been able to find elsewhere.

An example of this is Harriet. I first met with Harriet shortly after she lost her husband. She and her husband were high school sweethearts. Not having any children and having moved away from family, they were everything to one another. When he passed, she was left alone, felt depressed and missed him terribly. As a faithful woman, Harriet attended a support group hosted by her church designed for people who had lost their spouses. At first, her faith and the support group brought her comfort, but she still ached for her husband. More than that, she began to feel the support group, which continued to bemoan the losses of their spouses, held her back from finding peace. Lost and seeking something, anything, she attended a psychic fair in hopes of seeing a medium and connecting with her husband. That's where she met me. She sat down and he came through immediately. At the end of the session she walked away with tears streaming down her face, but those tears weren't from grief. They were tears of happiness. Harriet was smiling and standing taller than before.

That's not where this story ends, however. About

six months later, she came back. This time she had many questions, both for him and for me as to whether mediumship and intuition were against God's will. After our last session, having found such comfort in the reading, Harriet had shared her experience with her church group. Knowing it had helped her, she recommended that others speak to a medium as it might help them find some peace. Her recommendation was met with scripture warning her against psychics and mediums. It left her torn. She knew the peace she felt at having the opportunity to communicate with him that she hadn't been able to find anywhere else, but, she held the tenets of the Bible close to her heart. This is a challenge many face. And, when taken out of context, the Bible can be spun to make intuition, a relatively new concept, appear evil. That is not the case. Take 1 Corinthians 12: 8-11 for example:

"But the manifestation of the Spirit is given to every man to profit withal. For to one is given the Spirit the word wisdom; to another the word of knowledge by the same Spirit; To another faith by the same Spirit; to another the gifts of healing by the same Spirit; To another the working of miracles; to another prophecy; to another discerning of spirits; to another diverse kinds of tongues; to another the interpretation of tongues: But all these worketh that one and the selfsame Spirit, dividing to every man severally as he will.

In this verse, spiritual gifts such as mediumship and intuition are described as abilities that every individual has the opportunity of utilizing. These gifts are provided to us by God to assist us in better honoring him. This concept is explored further in 1 Corinthians 2: 9-10:

"What no eye has seen, what no ear has heard, and what no human has conceived" – *the thing God has*

prepared for those who love him – these are the things God has revealed to us by his Spirit.

And 1 Corinthians 9: 12-13:

What we have received is not the spirit of the world, but the Spirit who is from God, so that we may understand what God has freely given us. This is what we speak, not in words taught by human wisdom but in words taught by the Spirit, explaining spiritual realities with Spirit-taught words.

In both quotes, God provides each of us with wisdom. This wisdom is provided to help us become closer to him, closer to the mysteries of the greater universe. That is exactly what intuition facilitates and is the avenue through which this is accomplished.

Because intuition is a relatively new concept, the phrase first being coined in the 1600s but not coming into popular use until the late 1800s, it is referenced in the Bible as "discerning spirit" or "being led by Spirit." Instead of turning to these verses, those using scripture to discredit intuition turn to verses that reference "mediums," "witches" and "spiritism." If you review these verses, especially the most commonly cited verse Deuteronomy 18: 9-16, you will find that these verses are designed to convert individuals from their old, pagan ways and bring them into the new religion. You will also discover that the concept being warned against is not the message itself, rather who is delivering it and how that message is being portrayed. The Bible warns against mystics who deem themselves as a God or worse, above God. While infinite knowledge resides in each of us and each of us contains God within us, we are not The God. As stated in Proverbs 16:9, *"A man's heart deviseth the way: but the LORD directeth his steps."* Ultimately, it is my interpretation that as long as you don't put your faith in a medium, a psychic or yourself above God and the universe, you are not going against the Bible nor will you be punished for utilizing intuition.

The second reason people fear intuition: *The insights they receive are "bad."*

People who are naturally intuitive but who do not nurture their intuition tend to receive messages only when something catastrophic or life changing is about to happen. They may get a feeling when someone is about to die or an accident is about to occur. Or they might feel the distress from an individual who is being abused. If they are sensing spirits, more commonly referred to as ghosts, they are likely to feel the cranky, unhappy spirit that goes bump in the night rather than the loving grandparent that offers support. These feelings, be it from a ghost or the universe, bring pain. They bring discomfort. They bring bad news. And the feelings leave the recipient unnerved and not knowing what to do.

I experienced that disquiet a few years back. It was around Thanksgiving and I had a haunting feeling that someone was going to pass. I had no clue who and the nagging pang in my gut would not subside for weeks. I felt sick. I worried. Trying to quiet the discomfort, I attempted to convince myself that the feeling was an emotional remnant related to my grandfathers as both had passed on Thanksgiving. That didn't work. In continued efforts to minimize the feeling, I prepared myself for the passing of my grandmother or my husband's grandparents since all were elderly and ailing. That didn't work. The discomfort persevered. Then the day before Thanksgiving, we got the call. Todd had taken his life. Shock ran though me. I felt guilt.

To feel guilt upon receiving confirmation of a negative sign is not uncommon. Individuals question why, with this foreknowledge, weren't they able to change the outcome? Or did they not do something they were supposed to that would have changed the outcome? Guilt causes people to put the responsibility of the negative situation on their own shoulders. Using Todd as an example, I questioned why I didn't intuit more information that could have led to an intervention.

Whether we like it or not, in these situations what you must remember is that bad things do happen to good people. These unfavorable circumstances may provide the recipient with wisdom that could assist them in learning lessons they are here to learn. Knowing this rarely brings anyone any comfort. In fact, you may ask, "Wouldn't it be better not to know?" Perhaps, but in these situations intuition is supporting you in ways you don't even realize. The awareness may prepare you to handle the situation. For example, when Todd passed, I was better prepared to assist his family in coping with their grief. Or that feeling could cause you to take steps you might not have otherwise taken. While the actions didn't change the situation, these actions may facilitate closure and minimize regret. For example, the day before my Uncle Dennis passed, he called each of his siblings for the sole purpose of checking in. This behavior was out of character as Dennis did not routinely phone his siblings just to chat. At the time of the calls, he didn't know he was going to pass. He died suddenly and unexpectedly. I believe his intuition encouraged him and he felt driven to make the calls. I'm glad he did because even though we didn't talk, having the message on the answering machine provided comfort and helped us through our grief. That call may have been just as much for us as it was for him.

The silver lining is not always easy to find, especially while in the situation. In the moment, you will find yourself caught up in the frenzy and only able to see the heartache. And, to be quite honest, some situations are just lousy. For example, Todd's passing. There was nothing good about it. It was heart-wrenching. Taking care of his affairs was complicated and time-consuming. It was a horrible ordeal. My uncle's passing wasn't much better. Questions surrounded his passing. Due to an autopsy, the medical examiner held on to the body – which made the running family joke as my uncle was late to everything, "He'll be late for his own funeral" become a reality! In both these situations, the silver lining wasn't clear.

Fortunately, with time, you can look back and see that intuition helped the situation. What also helps is having absolute faith that what is meant to be, will be. Not everyone has that same belief. With that in mind, if every time you get a hunch it turns out to be devastating, it is no wonder it would cause fear!

That fear drives the question, *"Is this terrible situation my fault?"*

It is important to remember that through the messages you receive, while they may serve as a warning and may be a sign of bad news to come, you do not cause the bad news. For example, Todd didn't pass because I had a feeling someone was going to pass around Thanksgiving. If I were to claim it was my fault, any sane individual would assure me I was mistaken. He had his troubles. In no way was I a factor.

The same goes for you. If you receive a gut feeling that something bad is going to happen, it is not your fault. Believing that the fault is yours is both irrational and unfounded, but when an unpleasant situation occurs, you are often emotional and perhaps illogical, and you may believe you are to blame in some way. If you find that to be the case, pause and ask yourself these questions: Did I want this to happen? Could I have predicted this would occur? Is there anything I could have done to change the outcome? Chances are you will answer each question with a firm no.

Why? Because when we are faced with unexpected, devastating news, there is so much we still don't know. As discussed earlier, the mysteries of the universe are vast and hidden to us. That sign, that glimpse, is just one piece of a thousand-piece puzzle. You can't possibly know what it's going to look like when it's put together. You don't know everything.

Additionally, life was likened to a river in the last chapter. As we know, life takes unexpected twists and turns that ultimately lead us all to our end destination. If you are picking up on rough waters ahead, it is important to remember that the individual (you or someone else) may have chosen that path or the universe may be stepping in to assist the individual in accomplishing a life lesson. Either way, when you intuit information, you are just the messenger. As the messenger, unless it's your mail you aren't supposed to read it. Because it's not yours to read in its entirety, don't worry yourself with what was contained in the message. Have faith you are doing exactly what you are meant to do.

Having faith doesn't mean the situation will be any easier. Because as already indicated, intuition does bring bad news. *Intuition can be painful.*

Intuition can lead to headaches, backaches and ringing in the ears; it can cause you to feel nauseous or have chest pain; feel angry, depressed, anxious or fearful; some individuals have even experienced vomiting or diarrhea. Symptoms can be unpleasant. Despite the unpleasantness, you are encouraged not to fear the discomfort of your intuition. This discomfort is similar to a baby crying. While a baby crying can indicate pain, it more frequently indicates the need for attention, be it a bottle, new diaper, sleep, or snuggling. Discomfort caused by intuition, be it nausea or anxiety, is just an indication of an effort to get your attention.

Because of that, you are encouraged not to worry. The more you focus on your physical symptoms, the worse they become. We all know someone like that. Doreen is an example. Due to her chronic condition, she retired early. Her days now include sitting on the couch watching television and napping. She continuously complains about how much pain she is in and how terrible her life is. And her symptoms get worse. She gets better, however, when she visits family. The severity of her pain diminishes, her mood improves and she has more stamina. This is counterintuitive. You would think since she was pushing herself she would be worse, and she does worsen when it is mentioned. Observing this, some might say she is "faking" her symptoms. This could be true. More likely, her focus on her symptoms makes them seem worse than they are. Anything we focus on too long takes on a life of its own. That's why you are encouraged not to worry about those physical symptoms from intuition.

Instead, once in a calm state of mind, shift your attention from the pain and try to focus on the actual feeling. How do you do that? Focus on the pain. Then ask, "Is this pain physical?" Chances are your spiritual intuition will kick in and give you an answer instantaneously. If you feel "yes," see a doctor. Chances are you won't, so then ask, "What is it?" You'll be surprised at what your intuition tells you.

In doing this exercise, what was once perceived as physical or emotional pain will likely be replaced with a completely different and complex emotion. The emotion inappropriately perceived as fear or pain is what leads to the discomfort. Why? Because it is associated with something being wrong or broken. The complex feeling doesn't carry that same meaning.

Let's return to Todd to explain this further. As stated above, the thought of someone dying made me sick to my stomach. Once I turned away from the sick feeling and focused on the message that someone was going to pass, I no longer felt sick; rather, all I felt was certainty. There was no questioning that someone was going to pass. There wasn't even sadness that someone was going to pass, whereas, when I attempted to decipher the message focusing on the concept someone was going to die, only then did I develop a negative feeling in the pit of my stomach and worry swept over me. It wasn't the message; rather, it was how I interpreted and ultimately responded to that interpretation that brought discomfort.

Going to the root of those feelings is important because foreboding feelings may not result in something negative but might be positive. For example, one night while I was still living at home, I recall being awoken with the feeling that someone had forcefully tugged at my foot. Startled out of sleep, I was taken aback by a smell, much like burning rubber. Alarmed, my attention shifted to the rechargeable batteries sitting on my desk. I had plugged them in right before bed. To my surprise and alarm, small sparks were flying and the batteries were leaking. Had I not been awoken, who knows what could have occurred! To this day, I am uncertain what woke me from my sleep that night. Had I smelled the batteries burning and just not realized it until after I awoke? Was the universe trying to warn me that something was wrong? I don't know. And honestly, does it really matter? What matters was the message was received and I was safe. The discomfort from the message was worth it.

Warning, protecting and making our life as smooth as possible as we endeavor towards accomplishing our purpose is why we are intuitive. While we have talked about the negative, these feelings don't always have to be bad. Intuition is often good. Unfortunately, for those who do not look to or utilize their intuition, the negative feelings are what are most commonly experienced. Why? These energies of unpleasant situations tend to be more intense and intrusive than those of joy and happiness, making them easier to perceive. Envision it like this: negative feelings are shouted, whereas the positive feelings are whispered. It is easier to hear and comprehend the yell than the whisper.

The next reason people commonly fear and hence ignore their intuition is, *If I know things, other people do too. What are others intuiting about me?*

This fear is much less common, but it exists and it stems from a lack of confidence. Individuals who struggle with this fear often wonder, "What makes me so special?" "Why am I blessed with this gift?" While intuition is a skill everyone has, because mediumship and intuition have not been normalized, people continue to view the ability as a gift that is bestowed by God to only a select few. To these individuals, to be chosen as one of the special ones becomes overwhelming as they self-impose expectations of believing they should be holier, kinder and serve mankind.

Eventually, usually after attending development circles or talking with individuals, a shift in their perception occurs. They come to realize they aren't unique after all. They realize that everyone really is intuitive. This concept can be unnerving. Despite living in

ONE

a time where our lives are very public due to the use of social media, people still want to be private. They may post pictures of themselves and their families on Instagram, share their feelings on the latest trending topic on Twitter, and share intimate details into their latest escapades on Facebook, but these individuals have chosen what to share. These posts are often well thought out and represent an image of what they wish to portray, which is not necessarily a reflection of who they really are. We often do this without realizing it. Let's take Lee as an example. Lee, while in the company of his grandparents will not consume alcohol nor will he partake in any public displays of affection with his wife. Lee is thirty-six years old, has been married to his wife for ten years and has two kids. It's safe to assume his grandparents know he's having sex and has consumed alcohol at some point. When his wife asked him why he won't kiss her in front of his family, he didn't have an answer. Yet he doesn't feel comfortable. It is not the image he wishes to project.

Lee's behavior is inconsequential in the grand scheme of life, but it is representative of how important an individual deems the perception of others. Many of us have aspects of ourselves, be they things we've done that we are ashamed of or thoughts that run through our heads, that we do not want to share with others, even those closest to us. However, if all people are intuitive, that means that anyone can see past the façade to the truth of who someone is.

Knowing that people can see the real you can make you feel vulnerable and naked. The first time I walked into a psychic fair, that's the way I felt. I assumed everyone in the room could see my baggage, see my hurts and my desires. I also assumed everyone was casting judgments based on those observations, but you know what, I was wrong. Unless intuitives are offering insight, they don't care about your baggage and secrets. They have enough of their own!

Sadly, should you attend a development circle filled with like-minded and blossoming intuitives, you will at some point feel that vulnerability and someone will cause you to feel judged. This is rarely done purposely, and most of the time the trespasser is sharing unsolicited advice in hopes of being helpful. This energetic eavesdropper is likely excited by his or her newly found ability and eager to share it with everyone. Unfortunately, as the trespasser is still naïve and unseasoned, he or she will likely lack the tact and proper etiquette for approaching individuals with these newfound intuitive insights. I witness it all the time. It is part of the learning curve. You may even find yourself doing it. This will pass. As mentioned, the intuitive has enough of his own issues to resolve. Eventually your focus will be turned back on you.

This brings me to the final reason individuals fear intuition. *An individual sees who they really are.*

There comes a point in an individual's unique intuitive journey when he is forced to look behind the mask he wears and see who he is. With the mask removed, you can no longer pretend to be someone you're not. No lying. No hiding. No avoiding the tough questions. No trying to take the easy route or pass responsibilities onto others. Your intuition, that inner voice, knows the real you. And your inner voice will hold you to that.

Seeing yourself through an objective lens is hard. You will look back at your life and there will be things you regret, things you wish you had done differently. I know I do! When I've looked back on my own life, I recall a time when I was not kind to a classmate. The memory is vivid. I was in second grade. My birthday was coming up and my

ONE

parents were planning my party. My parents allowed me to invite all the girls in the class, but there was one classmate I didn't want to invite. Why didn't I want to invite her? Because she was not popular. That poor girl. Being left out! It haunts me to this day. I realize I can't change the past, but I can change the future, and you know what? I hope to never do that again. Instead, I strive for inclusion. As you review your life, be certain to be kind to yourself. No one is perfect. All you can hope is that you have learned from your mistakes.

Your unintentional and undesirable habits will also come into full view and may make you uncomfortable. An example of this is Peter. It was brought to Peter's attention a few years back that his humor can be off-putting. This was shocking to him as his jokes are mild mannered and usually politically correct. In fact, his jokes tend to be more punny than funny. But when his niece Paige got married, Peter realized not everyone was laughing at his jokes. He had hoped, and perhaps assumed, he would be asked to walk her down the aisle. Her father had passed as had her favorite uncle. She had few living male relatives with whom she was close. She didn't ask him and instead opted to walk down the aisle alone. Why? It turns out Paige thought Peter disliked her. This shocked him as he didn't think he had ever given her that impression. Where was the disconnect? Through the years, Peter told many dumb blonde jokes. Paige, a natural blonde, took them personally. When he heard this, he was heartbroken. It was by no means his intention to hurt her in any way, but he did. That was hard for him to accept. Again, he did. And, more importantly, he changed. Since then, I haven't heard a single blonde joke pass Peter's lips.

These are the types of realizations you will find yourself making. They are hard to accept. Many will likely be unintentional and you'll want to run from them. You'll wish you were ignorant and didn't know any better, but you will, and you will hold yourself to a higher standard. You will be willing to make the tough decisions. You will take responsibility. And you know what, life will be easier. And, more importantly, you will like yourself more. Why? Because you will be on the outside who you are on the inside.

ONE

CHAPTER EIGHT
HOW MESSAGES COME

"Synchronicity is an ever present reality for those who have eyes to see."
Carl Jung

Once you overcome the fear of intuition, you will become more aware of your intuition. You will notice all the synchronicities and coincidences you were blind to before. You will have feelings and insights you didn't observe before. Not only that, these insights will occur all the time, not as isolated, once-in-awhile occurrences.

At first, the feelings and synchronicities won't materialize on cue or at designated times. You won't have the ability to say, "I want to know about x" and receive a sign immediately. The signs will be subtle. They will not be the literal writing on the wall or telegrams with specific instructions. Nor will they be a booming voice from above firmly telling you which direction to take while a ray of light cuts through the darkness illuminating a path to joy. If you are expecting those type of signs, you are going to be waiting a very long time. Individuals, even the most gifted, rarely receive signs that are that obvious.

In fact, signs are rarely experienced with the senses of sight or sound. Observations made through the sights and sounds of physical and emotional intuition only provide the foundation and synchronicity for spiritual intuition to weave an intuitive message. Once woven, the intuitive message is commonly received via subtle and understated feelings.

What do these subtle and understated signs look and feel like? They are difficult to describe, as each individual's experience with them is slightly different. The common thread however, is they are random and they are unshakeable. Here are some examples of how the signs could be experienced:

- A feeling of your stomach being tied in a knot.
- Inexplicable heartache or heaviness in the chest.
- Ringing or buzzing in the ears.
- Warmth or coolness upon one's shoulders.
- Signs in the physical or dream world, i.e. a dead bird represents death to some whereas fish dreams indicate pregnancy for others.
- Sense of knowing without any explanation.

Because the intuitive feelings may be subtle, you at first may not consciously understand them. Subconsciously, you will understand the significance as the feelings will be nagging, stick with you longer, or you may find yourself coming back to the topic again and again. Due to this, you will continue to seek out answers.

Many of my clients are a great example of this. They will tell me, "I feel as though there is something I am meant to do. I just don't know what." Throughout our conversation, it turns out they do know the path they are being led towards. Their intuition has been prodding them through signs, friends and synchronicities. They just had a hard time putting the pieces together.

Let's explore this further with my client, Kristen. She came to me confused about her career. Throughout her session, messages indicated the time had come for her to move on from her position as she had come full circle. Turns out, Kristen had been feeling the same way. Not only that, a few weeks prior to our meeting she had literally come full circle. After enjoying an office with a window, due to an office reorganization, she found herself moved into the office she had when she started with the company ten years earlier. Kristen said the feeling she had at that time was that she was at the beginning of another cycle, yet, because she didn't have experience using her intuition, she, like many, had a hard time putting her feelings into words and thus appreciating the message. So, she came to me, but she didn't have to. Why? Because she could have put the pieces together herself. How? I'm going to tell you, but first, let's discuss the intuitive feelings that nudge you forward a little further. As mentioned earlier, these feelings are subtle. As such, they are unlikely to lie at the ends of the emotional spectrum such as happiness or sadness, anger or joy, fear or love. Rather, they are moderate emotions such as confidence, tranquility or apprehension. They are the emotions that drive you towards the emotions at the ends of the spectrum.

To recognize and, more importantly, understand the subtle messages provided by moderate emotions, you must change the way you think. If you are like many in today's age, you use a limited vocabulary broadly categorizing situations as good or bad, black or white, and happy or sad. By using these sweeping categories, emotions and resulting signs are limited. Life's purpose is not one of pure happiness or sadness. Your path will bring you great joy and sorrow, and along the way you are going to feel all the emotions on the spectrum. Every step you take along the way will be complex, not simply right or wrong. For example, when taking a job, you will feel excitement regarding the opportunities afforded by the new position. At the same time, you may feel vulnerable for you don't know anyone at the new position and you are taking on a lot of new responsibilities. You may also feel nostalgic while reflecting on the friendships you will be leaving. Not only that, you may feel resentment towards your boss because he didn't fight harder to keep you. Many emotions, all at once. This complexity occurs in every situation. As your intuition communicates with you to prepare you for this journey, you will experience all these feelings. That's why your intuition may feel confusing, unclear or even contradictory. By pausing and paying attention to the nuances, the signs become more defined.

To assist the universe in providing you with defined messages, it helps to be familiar with the subtleties of your emotions. Here is an exercise to try.

Exercise 5
Identifying Emotions

Before starting this exercise, take a moment to review the list of emotions outlined in Appendix A. After reviewing the list of emotions, choose four: two positive and two negative. Two of those emotions you should be less familiar with.

Next, go to a dictionary and look up the meaning of each emotion. Does the definition of that emotion fit your understanding of the word? You may be surprised that the definition may be slightly different than you assumed. Which of the emotions is the most positive? Sit and reflect upon this emotion's definition. Do you have a memory that could be described by this emotion? If not, imagine a situation that would create this feeling. As you think about this memory or situation, vividly see, hear and feel the circumstance play out. While thinking about the situation, allow the emotion to flood over you. Imagine you are in that moment, feeling that emotion for the first time. You may laugh. You may cry. You may become angry. Allow yourself to. The imagined circumstance will likely contain multiple emotions, so try to focus your attention only on the emotion at hand. After living through the memory, jot down any thoughts that remain regarding the emotion.

Repeat this exercise by moving to the most negative emotion, then the lesser of the negative emotions and finally the lesser of the positive emotions. Repeat this exercise until you have completed it for all the terms in Appendix A.

Additionally, you are encouraged to use these terms in conversation. Use them to describe how you are feeling as opposed to using sweeping generalizations. By doing this, the meanings will not only be cemented in your mind, but the feelings of those emotions will be as well. This gives the universe a larger language through which to communicate with you.

Creating a more diverse language for the universe to communicate with you is beneficial because communicating with the universe is a little like charades. If you've ever played charades, you know you will do anything to get your point across and help your teammate figure out the answer. The more attuned a team is, the easier it becomes. For example, if your teammate loves movies and tries using current movie references to jog your memory but you haven't seen a new movie in five years, it's going to be a very frustrating game. However, if you both love sports and use that shared language, the frustration is minimized. The same thing applies in terms of a shared language with the universe.

To further diversify the language through which you communicate with the universe, in addition to practicing the emotion exercise, you are encouraged to begin to create your own personal symbolism dictionary. People do this all the time when a loved one passes. They will have a specific sign, be it a cardinal, butterfly or pennies, that represents their loved one. When they see the sign, they are reassured their family member is watching over them. In the next exercise, you will be doing the same thing, only instead of identifying a sign for a loved one, you will be assigning signs through which the universe can provide you with insight.

Exercise 6
Signs from the Universe

Get a piece of paper. Fold the paper in thirds. On the top one third write, "Yes." On the second third write, "No." And on the third section write, "Undecided." Begin thinking about what signs you might want to receive. Your signs can be anything. You can have an animal such as a bear or eagle. You ask for a word, phrase or song. You are only limited by your own imagination. For example, my friend uses an "X" for no and I use a hawk for yes. The only recommendations I have while you are choosing your signs are: pick a sign that is rare enough that you won't see or hear it everywhere, i.e. don't pick the number one song on the music charts; but at the same time, choose a sign that is common enough that it won't be impossible for it to appear, i.e. don't pick a purple giraffe wearing a pink tutu, big earrings and very red lipstick.

After you've brainstormed a few ideas, jot down two or three in each category. Close your eyes and visualize each one of the symbols. Are there ones you just can't see? If so, cross them off your list. The three that are easiest for you to see in your head and feel in your heart, keep. One should remain in each category. We are going to use them.

Now is the fun part. Start using them. At first, you are just going to prove to yourself that the universe will provide you with signs. Don't ask any questions yet. Instead, choose a specific length of time; my recommendation is twenty-four to seventy-two hours. Then choose a specified number of times you'd like to see the signs. Ask for the chosen symbols to be shown in the time frame and the specified number of times. Then wait.

The symbols may pop up immediately. They may all appear in the twenty-third hour. Wait. Be patient. Most importantly, be open-minded. It is not uncommon for the symbols to appear in an unexpected way. For example, you ask for pennies and instead of finding coins, you meet three people named Penny. And while rare, you may find one of the symbols you brainstormed but didn't select pops up. Add that to your list; use that too!

Now that your symbols are popping up, let's test the validity of their meaning. Have someone ask you a question that they know the answer to but you don't. Then wait for the signs. You might have a sign pop into your head immediately or you might have to wait. If you don't want to wait for the answer, you can look for it. Go on Facebook or flip through a magazine. Does one of your symbols pop up? Once you get the sign, confirm you received the correct sign.

If you received the incorrect sign, remind yourself and the universe of your symbols and try again. If you got the right answer, keep playing! Know that you may not get the "right" answer all the time. The more you practice, the closer you will get to 100%.

It's also important to note that you are not limited to Yes, No, and Undecided. If you would like to expand your dictionary, continue to assign symbols to meanings. You are only limited by your own imagination.

By creating your dictionary and enhancing your feelings, you and the universe are beginning to work together as a team, because as in charades, the actor, or in this case, the universe, knows the answer. It is through its actions that it helps its teammate, you, get to the correct answer. Again as in charades, this only works if both members on some level know the answer. For example, if in charades your teammate is given the book *Of Mice and Men* and one or both of you don't know the book, it would be very hard to communicate that. Fortunately, it is guaranteed that on some level you know the answer. You may not realize you know the answer, but the universe will help you see that information and connect the dots.

An example of this can be related to a tree on my property. My husband and I bought our home knowing at some point the massive tree, which literally takes three people to get their arms around, would need to be trimmed if not removed. The home inspector pointed out that one limb was pushing on the garage. He also noted that at some point one of the previous owners must have intended to remove the limb because a cut line had been put on the tree.

After purchasing the house, my husband contacted several tree services for quotes for both removing the limb and taking the whole tree out. The quotes came back from $2,500 - $5,000 for the limb and up to $20,000 for the entire tree. At the time, we decided to risk it. Years went by and the tree continued to grow. Then the garage began to lean. Around that time, I began to have nightmares and day visions of the massive branch coming down. Still unwilling to bite the bullet and take care of the limb, I had my husband move anything of value out of the garage. Not only that, we opted to park the car out of harm's way at the very end of our driveway.

The feeling the limb was going to come down continued to nag me. And then, a limb did come down: not the big one but a sizable one nonetheless. I could have dismissed my feelings and told myself, "That's what I'd been worried about." I didn't though; I knew better and didn't need to be told twice. That day we decided to have the tree taken care of. In this situation, we knew full well the tree was a problem. The universe didn't need to inform us of that. The home inspector and our leaning garage were evidence enough. That nagging feeling as well as the limb falling, however, were how the universe spoke to me. I felt the concern, and I witnessed the weakness of the tree. That was the sign I needed.

By this point you are probably amazed at all the different ways messages come. Some are clear and apparent, like that of the limb falling. Many more are the feelings or the intuitive knowledge, like the nagging worry. Either of those by themselves were not enough for me to get the sign. It was the repetition and the synchronicities that assisted me and will assist you in connecting the dots.

Synchronicities have been mentioned a few times so far. Because they are a way the universe communicates, let's take a moment to define what they are. First described by Carl Jung, synchronicity is a theory that asserts that two seemingly unrelated and coincidental events are in fact connected in some manner but that connection cannot yet be explained in a logical fashion. For example, you are considering going to tonight's football game. In a synchronous situation, a friend would call you up, without provocation, with tickets to said game and invite you to go with him or her.

Synchronicity happens all the time. In fact, it was how my husband and I chose the venue for our wedding. My husband proposed while we were on vacation in early June. Knowing both his and my family would be visiting during the same week in late August, we decided to keep our engagement short and get married then. This left us with a little more than two months to plan the affair. With a lot to plan, we took the opportunity during our long car ride home to discuss details. We concluded we wanted to have the event at a winery. Coincidentally, a flyer from a winery advertising their wedding venue was in our mailbox when we arrived home. Perfect placement. We embraced that sign and had our event there.

Embracing the synchronicity right away, as my husband and I did, is rare. Why? Because most individuals, myself included, don't get or don't believe the message the first time it is presented. Rather, individuals want to be sure they aren't "making it up." This reason is why signs are repetitious in nature. And synchronicity is the universe's way of accomplishing the repetition. I know, even I am being repetitious, but by being repetitious you, the person receiving the information, will have more opportunity to notice the sign, understand the underlying reason for that message and be assured you are interpreting the message appropriately. Until you are assured and take consequent action, the message will keep coming.

Synchronicity and repetition are the reason your life carries a theme. The theme might come from the wisdom and insight of your friends, family or even strangers. Or you might be hearing the message in songs or on billboards. Or you might find the same type of people or circumstances continue to pop up. Whatever form it comes in, it comes again and again and again. These instances have been put in your path to trigger a thought or affirm a desire that may already exist. For example, when my husband was considering a degree in metaphysics, the university he was interested in came up in conversation no less than five times. In a situation like that, it is time to pause and take notice.

Hopefully it has become clear that messages come in a variety of shapes and sizes to cause you to pause, take notice, and ultimately be guided. As the word "guide" suggests, the messages don't force action upon you. You are the one who ultimately chooses which direction and actions to take. No matter what direction you take, the universe will support you.

CHAPTER NINE
HELPING YOU ACHIEVE YOUR LIFE'S PURPOSE

"Follow your heart and intuition. They somehow already know what you want to become."
Steve Jobs

Why is the universe so intent on helping you out? Just like the tree that plays its role by transforming carbon dioxide back into oxygen providing all mammals oxygen to breathe or the bacteria that grow unnoticed in your gut but assist in the digestion of your food or the fruits and vegetables that bring us nourishment, you were born into this world with a specific purpose. The role you play, the actions you take, and the lessons you learn keep the world turning. Without you, the world would be thrown off kilter. It is for that reason the universe steps in to help you. The better you are, the more capable you are in playing that role.

While we all have a role to play, not every aspect of your life is destined. You have free will and the ability to choose your own path. This path, which some believe we come into this world to follow, I will refer to as a blueprint or contract.

Let's talk about this contract for a moment. The blueprint outlines the lessons your soul intends to learn

ONE

during this lifetime. Think of your contract as a strategic plan. It includes a vision and mission as well as long term intended outcomes. The activities and tactics that will be implemented to achieve those intended outcomes are not included in the plan. That is where free will comes in.

Likening your contract to a strategic plan, your vision is your soul's purpose. The soul's purpose is greater than yourself and is what, in the Kabbalah, is whispered into the baby's ear. Unfortunately, once born, the clarity of that vision is obscured; thus knowing, let alone understanding, the soul's purpose while alive is hard to do. The soul knows it, but the conscious mind does not. You may get glimpses now and again, but those glimpses are brief. Why? Because this vision is like the Earth. You can only see the Earth from where you are standing at any given moment, which is limited to only as far as the eye can see. To fully understand the vision, you would have to not only see the Earth from space, but visit every city, town, nook and cranny. It's the big picture. While ill-equipped to fully take the full meaning in while alive, you will get glimpses of this wisdom throughout your life.

Seeing the vision of your own life is hard, just as calculus can be challenging for someone who has not gotten past basic geometry. A further complication is that your life is not lived in isolation. You are only one player in the bigger picture that is the universe. This would be like trying to understand not only calculus but also organic chemistry, which requires understanding of calculus. This is challenging, if not impossible. And then apply that to each individual and take into consideration the butterfly effect. It becomes more complicated by the moment. That's one of the reasons why understanding all the ways your actions are impacting the whole is challenging.

Not only that, can you imagine if you knew and could see all the outcomes and consequences of each individual action? You'd be overwhelmed by the impact you are making on the world – for good and for bad. Seeing the ripple effect and knowing that each decision you make has not a small, but big impact on the world could cause you to worry you might screw something up or hurt someone. This feeling of responsibility (which is as unfounded as the fear discussed in Chapter 7 about getting a feeling the negative outcome is your fault) may cause heartache and inaction. There are times ignorance is bliss, and this is one of those times. And that is another reason the vision is hidden from you.

It is also hidden because if you did have all the knowledge, you might not go through struggles that would help you learn important life lessons. Those struggles wouldn't be as deep. That is why other than glimpses of your soul's purpose, you will be searching throughout your life.

What you can begin to understand, however, is one's mission or life purpose. Unlike the soul's purpose, which is greater than you, your life purpose is limited to you. Think of it this way, your life purpose is one book in a series, whereas your soul's purpose is the tale that is carried out throughout the series.

Your life purpose outlines what you are meant to learn during this life. By understanding this more fully, you are able to overcome the obstacles you face more easily. You may now be thinking, "Great! How do I understand my purpose more?" It's easy. Through reflection. By taking the time to reflect on your life, you can understand more about yourself and identify your life theme, which will provide you with insight as to why you respond to circumstances the way that you do.

What is a life theme? Psychologists also refer to life themes as archetypes. First imagined by Sigmund Freud and Carl Jung, the archetypes have been explored by many, including Joseph Campbell and most recently, Carol Pearson. She conducted in-depth and expansive research narrowing the archetypes down to the following twelve: the Innocent, the Orphan, the Warrior, the Caregiver, the Seeker, the Lover, the Destroyer, the Creator, the Jester, the Sage, the Magician, and, the Ruler.[7] Life themes not only help explain your personality and behaviors but also the situations and experiences you have throughout your life. As the name suggests, the theme occurs again and again throughout your life and gives insight as to your life purpose.

Curious as to what your life theme may be? You may already have an inkling. If not, the following exercise is designed to assist you in discovering it.

Exercise 7
Discovering Your Life Theme

Sit back and reflect on your life. Start from today and work your way back. What were the most profound moments or important lessons you experienced in the last year? In no particular order, write them down. Allow your mind to wander through the past twelve months, jotting down moments of pain and joy.

Once you have gone back through the past year, allow your mind to reflect back over the last five years. What were the most significant moments? As you roam through the last five years, what memories jump into your mind most vividly? They may be good. They may be bad. You may find your thoughts revolve around a person or place.

Jot those down. Write down the memories and lessons you want to remember. Also, write down the ones you wish you could forget.

Continue this exercise thinking back over the last ten years and continue working your way back through your lifetime in ten year intervals until you get to college, high school, middle and elementary school. Do those separately. Lastly, wander throughout your entire lifespan one last time and jot down any other memories and lessons you may have overlooked.

The review of your life could be done in one or several sittings. The choice is yours and no one way is better than another. Once you have reflected over the entirety of your lifetime and have created a robust list of memories, take the time to review and rank those memories and lessons. Those memories that are more vivid, both in detail and emotion, should be ranked the highest.

Now look only at the top ten to twelve memories on your list. Why are these memories important to you? How are the memories alike? Are there similar players in each of them? Do you play a similar role? Or perhaps you learn a similar lesson? What makes you happy in each of these memories? Similarly, what brings you stress regarding these memories? As you ask these questions, you will find many similarities occur in each situation. In this short list, you may find there are outliers, memories that don't cleanly fit into the theme of the other. That's ok! They are supporting who you are today.

Now turn to Appendix B to review the life themes. What theme correlates to your experiences? You've just found your life theme!

ONE

In doing the exercise, what trends did you see appear again and again? For me, it should come as no surprise, that when I did this exercise I found the majority of my memories involved spiritual components. For example, after my grandfather died, I remember listening to his cousin Eugene speak of a circle of pearls he saw floating around my grandfather's head. For Eugene, this signified my grandfather was going to die. And I remember standing up proudly in middle school to talk about my Indian Guide. In college, I remember learning all the college's ghost stories, only to recount them on every single tour I gave of the campus. I even met my husband on a ghost hunt! The list goes on and on. Because of that, I initially thought: "I must be the Sage." But on further exploration, I found an important aspect in each of these memories I didn't expect to find. Each memory involved sharing lessons or teaching to create change – something I am passionate about. After further reflection, I believe my archetype is not the Sage but rather the Magician. I encourage you to take time to do this exercise and look deeper than just the surface. You may be surprised by what you stumble upon, just like I was.

You may, as I did, find that several themes fit. And they may. Because while you have one life theme, the other life themes support that primary mission. Nothing in life is black and white, one category or another. If you struggle, first toss out of your mind what it is you want to be. I wanted to be the sage. You may want to be the caregiver. Then reexamine the meanings of each archetype. Which one feels right? Trust your intuition, you will probably know. If you don't, use your symbols. That's what they are there for after all! Got your life theme? Good! Let's move on.

Understanding your life theme is important because it gives you greater insight into just what your soul and life purpose or mission and vision are, just as in a strategic plan understanding the mission and vision keeps a person on track. So can knowing one's theme. It gives you a greater understanding as to why a situation may be occurring, hence making the lessons you learn and the knowledge you accumulate throughout your lifetime make more sense. As opposed to random situations that happen to you, it gives you a construct as for why things are happening and why you are responding to a situation the way you are. With this understanding, it also helps you break the cycle of continuously finding yourself in the same situation and circumstance. You will have learned the lesson and will be able to move on to the next.

For example, throughout my life I have often found myself rarely in the lead but rather in supporting roles. As a child, rather than being the team leader, I was the individual voted by my teammates as most spirited. In college, I was not the President of my sorority; rather, I took supporting roles in recruitment and member education. In my corporate position, I was the behind-the-scenes right hand of the organizational leader. And, to be honest I didn't mind these roles. All of them played into the life theme of Magician. As the team player, I knew that I had an important job that needed to be done and that by doing it I was helping create the vision the team, the sorority and the organization had in mind. I saw magic happen.

But then something changed. When I left my full-time corporate job to pursue a career as a medium, author and speaker full time, I was lost. I was the team player without a team. The skills I had developed as a team player were no longer serving me, which led me to worry:

"What did I do?" Trying to fix the feeling of being lost, I tried to create a team and collaborate. I partnered with one person after another. These partnerships didn't go well. Why? Because I continued to try to play a supporting role, but it was no longer time for me to be the assistant. It was time for me to be the leader and manifest my visions, not someone else's. This was a new lesson for me to learn. Since then I have realized that life is "easy" again. Recognition is more than half the battle.

Wondering what your big life lessons are? Let's walk through this exercise.

Exercise 8
Discovering Your Life Lessons

Pull out that list of memories you created in the Discovering Your Life Theme exercise. Choose one memory and think about who you were before the happy moment or the lesson that was learned. Close your eyes and picture yourself. Remember your hairstyle and clothing choices. Hear the music you jammed out to at the time playing in your head. More importantly, reflect on the person you were: your hopes and fears, your ego and insecurities, as well as your values and beliefs. Remember who you were before the situation. Then reflect on who you were during the experience and following it. What about you changed? How are you different? What lessons did you learn?

For example, one of the most influential moments in your life may have been the marriage to your spouse. If you aren't married, perhaps reflect on an influential friendship. Think about who you were before you met that person. If you had met him or her earlier in your life,

> would the two of you have gotten along? Why or why not? What about you had to change? What about you is different now that he or she is in your life? How are you better for the relationship? What lessons are you still learning?
>
> Complete this exercise for a few of the influential moments of your life. Do you see a theme occurring? Most likely! Now take that theme and look at your life today, specifically the places where you are feeling stressed, overwhelmed and dissatisfied. Then apply this theme, these lessons to the situation. Viewing the situation in those terms, are you able to find a solution? A tactic that might release the situation?

What you may see, much like the themes, is that life lessons repeat themselves throughout our lives. This happens because although you may work through the lesson once, in life you must practice towards perfecting that lesson. For example, the violinist doesn't play through a piece once without error and then put it down. Rather, the violinist continues practicing to perfect that piece and add flair, making the piece better than initially imagined. The same is true for life lessons. You add your flair. Fortunately, by identifying struggles, it makes it easier to move through them. It also makes it easier for you to accept assistance from the universe.

You may be thinking, "If my life themes and lessons are already determined and I don't know them but the universe does, should I just let the universe take over?" If this thought is running through your head, you might be sitting back and waiting for your symbols, doing nothing. I encourage you to go back and reread Chapter 6. Don't sit back and wait. Intuition is about actively engaging with the energies around you. Unfortunately, too many individuals awakening spiritually do sit back and wait. It never goes well. Each of us has lessons to learn. When people become complacent and unwilling to make decisions, they halt their personal growth and find themselves running in circles. Unfortunately, as mentioned earlier, indecision is a decision. It's a decision without any of the action. In life, you need to take the action and do the work. Work results in life lessons. The universe doesn't have control over what happens, only you do. That's why understanding your life theme and life lessons is so important. And over time they do become easier.

    An example of this is Angela. She was unhappy in her marriage and wanted to leave but wasn't certain it was the right decision. She informed me she was waiting for a sign to confirm it was time. She waited for a year. And then another. Knowing that her husband was verbally abusive and had become financially irresponsible, I asked her what "sign" she was looking for. After stammering for a moment, Angela admitted she didn't know, she thought it would be something very clear as opposed to this slow and continual decline. I encouraged her to ask for a specific sign and take control of the situation. She did. And you know what? Angela got the symbol immediately! The universe is there to help, it wants to help. Helping you helps it. But again, it is only through nudges, rarely through action. So now let's talk about how you help the universe help you.

SECTION THREE
WORKING WITH THE UNIVERSE

ONE

CHAPTER 10
TRUST

"Trust your instincts. Intuition doesn't lie."
Oprah Winfrey

The first and most important way to strengthen your intuition is through Trust. Think back to a time at work you felt overwhelmed, as though the weight of the world was on your shoulders. Was it? Or did you have colleagues that could have assisted had you only leaned on them? There are probably many times in your life you opted to complete a task by yourself rather than asking for help. Unfortunately, your loved ones and colleagues can't assist you if you don't ask. Nor can the universe. If you don't ask for assistance, you may or may not get it. And if you do ask, you have to trust that its actions are in your best interest. With trust, magic happens.

Trust, which ultimately results in faith, is not something that is easily gained. You have years of disappointment when life hasn't gone your way. Not only that, we live in a society where perfection is idolized. Striving for perfection, rather than finding the positive attributes of a situation, we are constructively critical, at best, as to how the situation could have been handled better. At worst, we become cynical and believe the situation was bound to fail from the get-go.

ONE

Intuitives, however, tend to see things a little differently. Rather than being critical, an intuitive finds the silver lining, the lesson learned and the opportunity for improvement. It is a characteristic all intuitives strive for. They trust and have faith that life will be okay. This mindset is hard to teach. As mentioned, society has ingrained an unrealistic mindset to strive towards perfection, an impossibility. Breaking that mindset is challenging. I can't do it for you. Your friend can't do it for you. The only one who can do it is you. Fortunately, supplied below are some tips on how to increase your faith and trust in the universe.

First and foremost you must believe, in every single cell of your body, that there is something bigger than you out there. Not only that, you must embrace that belief. How do you develop and embrace this belief? With education. Pick up every self-help, psychology, inspirational, religious even scientific text you can get your hands on. Whether you realize it or not, by picking up this book you have already started!

Why is educating yourself important? There is a saying that states, "Thoughts become words, words become actions, actions become beliefs, and beliefs ultimately become truths." By educating yourself, you are supplying your mind which is programmed to look at data and facts to better understand the world, with information. Like a sponge, your mind will soak up this information that will then become thoughts. The more you read, the more thoughts you will have that support trust in the universe. As you become more confident in those thoughts, they will become the words that fill the conversations with your friends and family. And, eventually, those thoughts and words will turn into actions, beliefs and ultimately, trust.

TRUST

If you have been practicing the exercises in this book, you have completed step two, which is to practice communication with the universe. Practice could be done in the quiet of your own home through meditation. Or, if you prefer to practice with like-minded individuals, you could join a group, often called a circle, to converse on spiritual topics or practice the skills you have learned.

Just like in any other ability, practice hones your skill. Think of the ballerina who practices for endless hours until her feet are blue and tired. She trusts that due to the practice her body will take over during the performance. Similarly, the intuitive trusts that the time practicing will have strengthened connection and the signs will be there when needed. Practice creates trust.

To demonstrate the importance of practice, let me share the story of two students, Nadine and Sean. They both joined my class around the same time. At the onset, I would have told you they came to the class at about the same developmental level, as both had taken previous classes and were receiving intuitive messages. Both attended all the sessions and participated equally in class, but that is where the similarity ends. Nadine would take the exercises provided in class, go home and practice every day. She would also come prepared with questions and ask for additional exercises. Sean did not. He practiced only during the three hours we met each month. Once he left, the information he had just learned did not come up until the next month.

After a year of training, Nadine was leaps and bounds ahead of Sean. She was receiving inspiration every day, several times a day. She was even practicing in the community. Sean, unfortunately, was at approximately the same place he started. He was frustrated. He didn't understand why Nadine had blossomed and he had not.

Not only that, because he wasn't receiving the signs as clearly as his peers, he trusted it less. The point of this story is, if you don't practice, the universe can't prove to you that it is working for and with you.

It is important to note that the trust obtained through practice is not just in the universe and the signs the universe provides. Rather, you will also learn to trust yourself. Intuition, for better and for worse, has a stigma of being an extraordinary "gift." Individuals often have a hard time seeing themselves as special and doubt their intuition. Through practice, the universe demonstrates that you really are receiving messages, which in turn causes you to realize that (extra)ordinary you has the ability. This is important because until you realize this, no matter how many signs you are provided with, you will miss them. This was the case with Kellie.

She has been on the spiritual path for a long time. In fact, I met her before I started working in this field and was taking classes. At the time, Kellie doubted herself and she grew slowly, but she was committed. And while she didn't trust herself, Kellie's faith remained strong and steadfast. She trusts the universe more than anyone I have ever met. Due to her trust in the universe, over the years Kellie has continued to take classes. In fact, when I started teaching, she decided to attend classes with me. The block continued, but then something changed. If you ask her, she'd tell you it is because I'm such a good teacher. While I am honored by that and wish I could take the credit, I did not create the change. Kellie created the change in herself. She found time. She meditates every day. Sometimes for just for five minutes. See, practice does work! And more importantly, she stopped doubting the signs she was getting. Before, she would get one of her symbols and dismiss it and tell herself she was making it up. Kellie doesn't do that anymore. As a result, she gets signs daily. And they are becoming stronger. What was once just little flickers of light and singular words, are now colors, sentences and feelings. And these signs don't just happen when she meditates or she asks. She has gotten them while riding her bike, washing the dishes, even while at work. When she gets them, she pauses and recognizes the messages for what they are.

Practice to create trust in the universe and yourself takes time. Once you start getting the signs, you will be like Kellie and see them everywhere, all the time. You might even feel like you want to tell the universe to cool it!

The next step in developing trust is the most difficult. In fact, many people, even some professional psychics, mediums and healers I know haven't done this. What is it? You share your beliefs with your friends, family, and even strangers.

Sharing one's beliefs is a frightening concept. A stigma around intuition exists. This stigma was discussed at length in Chapter 7 and exists even in many of the believers. It's true! While teaching a class on Business Tools for the Metaphysician, I had one woman tell me: "Dawn, I can't have a Facebook page. The people I work for can't know I read Tarot." Another time a colleague said, "The holidays are always interesting, if only my family knew what I do!" These statements are from people doing the work who have already fought through some of the stigma. For you, perhaps at the beginning of your journey, it is likely even more daunting, but once you share your belief and remove the mask, it is empowering.

To help in sharing your beliefs with individuals, especially non-believers and cynics, here are some things to consider.

ONE

Be prepared to address a non-believer's fear. Re-read Chapter 7 and enter the discussion about faith armed with some of the arguments to dismiss his or her fear. It has been my experience that many non-believers don't truly not believe, but rather they are afraid of the implications of intuition. Addressing those fears is the first step to breaking down the wall of cynicism.

The second step comes when the non-believer questions your "blind" trust and faith. You may encounter some skeptics who will propose that the reason you see signs everywhere is that you are predisposed to looking for the signs. He or she will argue that you are not truly an objective observer and that you see the signs because you want to see the signs. The naysayer does have a point. If you are looking for something, you are more likely to find it or make connections one might not normally make. Now I choose to believe these signs are a force greater than ourselves, but, let's play devil's advocate for a moment. Even if it isn't the universe, if these supposed signs give you hope and lead you down a path that brings you happiness, does it really matter? If the non-believer is open to the symbol exercise, demonstrate that. If not, smile and leave it at your knowing the signs make you happy.

Other naysayers, particularly the religious ones, will tell you they are worried about your eternal soul and/or that you are going to be attacked by demons. If you have gone through steps one and two, educated yourself and practiced, their concerns should be laughable. If this objection bothers you, my recommendation is to educate yourself further and educate them, if they are open to it.

The most challenging obstacle you must overcome regarding skeptics has less to do with the objections they raise and more to do with you. In embracing your intuition and trusting it enough to share with others, you will likely find that you are "afraid" of what others will think of you. Will skeptics think you are foolish or gullible? Will they think less of you or be offended by your beliefs? This fear is bringing to the surface your own skepticism and doubt. Ironically, your discomfort in sharing your beliefs and trust in the universe opens the door for more skepticism. If you aren't comfortable in your own skin, how is anyone else, especially a skeptic, supposed to be accepting of your belief system?

By forcing yourself into the uncomfortable position of sharing your faith with others, this moves you from the realm of thoughts to that of words and actions. This moves you closer to having a new truth. Truths are unshakeable and easy to have trust in. Once intuition becomes your truth, you can't help but trust it. Sharing is a leap, but once you take it, there is no going back.

This was the case with Toni. Incredibly intuitive, Toni came to my classes because she felt energy around, her but she was unclear as to why or how to use it. A dutiful student, she worked through the exercises and found the creation of a dictionary of symbols especially helpful, but Toni was still struggling with her gift. Messages didn't come on cue; in fact, there were many times she would ask for a message and was met with silence. When the messages did come, they were urgent and forceful. She doubted herself and her interpretation, that is until she started sharing her gift with others. Toni started by doing Tarot readings for friends. Soon she found herself starting conversations about spirituality with strangers. She even informed her father, a huge skeptic, that this is who she is… and he accepted it. Through sharing, she realized a part of her was still afraid and wasn't completely open. Once she shared, she became

ONE

accountable to herself and her beliefs. Since then, the messages have been clearer and more consistent. She has trust in herself and it shows.

So, while trust is hard and it will take time, by taking the simple steps of educating, practicing and sharing, you increase your trust in the universe and, more importantly, yourself. Once you do that, the messages will flow.

CHAPTER 11
EGO

"The moment you become aware of the ego in you, it is strictly speaking no longer the ego, but just an old, unconditioned mind-pattern. Ego implies unawareness. Awareness and ego cannot coexist."
Eckhart Tolle

Once you trust your intuition, the next step in successfully utilizing your intuition is keeping the ego in check. The ego is that nagging voice in your head that reminds you of the lessons you have learned, the experiences you have had, and the core beliefs you have developed from your unique set of life experiences. Many associate ego with arrogant or overly confident behavior. And it is, but it is more than that. The ego also creates fear and causes doubt. For the ego likes the status quo. Change can result in hurt and disappointment, something the ego does not like and works hard to avoid.

If you are sitting there thinking, "I don't have an ego. I don't need to read this chapter," you should read this chapter not once, but twice, because you are wrong. Everyone has an ego. Think about it for a moment. How old are you? The older you are, the more experiences you have had and the more ego you must overcome. Think

ONE

about all the experiences you have had over your lifetime: from the first time you won a game to the first time a friend disappointed you to your last illness and even the time you were passed over for a job by someone who was less experienced or less qualified than yourself. Each of these experiences equates to lessons learned that have become your truths and beliefs. These truths and beliefs have formulated your ego, for good and for bad. These truths reside deep within you.

And while ego is usually considered negative, having an ego isn't necessarily a bad thing. The ego can provide you with valuable insight. It reminds you of your history, your family's history and your culture's history. By reminding you of this past, it assists in keeping you safe and avoiding the mistakes you and others have made before. There are a lot of lessons in the ego, but in this effort to keep you safe, ego often creates fear. It elicits righteousness. Creating these negative situations is where it becomes problematic and can stunt your personal growth. It is also through fear and righteousness that your intuition will be drowned out.

The struggle you will face with the ego will be much like an addiction. The ego will make you feel good. It will tell you what you want to hear. It will even supply you with facts and what you perceive to be insights that support what you want to hear, but it is not real. The lies it tells you will not change your life, help you learn life lessons or make you happy. And like an addict, even though you may not have drunk from the well of ego for a week, a month, a year, five years – the struggle not to take a drink will be with you every day.

No one is immune to this battle. And the struggle you face as you become more intuitive will become greater. Ego, and the fear it creates, is something we all struggle with. This includes me. One place I am especially mindful of my ego is in the field of psychology. Interested in why individuals behave the way they do, I studied psychology in college. Early on, I recognized that I wasn't fond of the teachings of Sigmund Freud or Alfred Adler, where the focus was on talking out one's problems. Rather, I was drawn to branches of psychology that were supported by, even loosely, science and cause/effect relationships. I wanted to see how clear, actionable steps could be formulated to modify behavior. My role models were Ivan Pavlov, B.F. Skinner and Albert Bandura.

Having a preference as I did for one form of psychology or another is not a bad thing. It is what makes each of us unique. This is not ego. Rather, ego is your viewing your preference as better than another's, your trying to force your preference upon another, or your finding yourself judging people who hold an opinion different than yours.

The ego's judgment of others for having different opinions than our own is something everyone has, usually unconsciously. It might be a thought that crosses your mind such as, "I thought she was smarter than that." It could be an action, such as unfriending people on Facebook because of the viewpoints they hold and post about. It could be rolling your eyes at someone as they speak and then talking to them in a condescending tone because you don't agree with their opinion. It could even be passive aggressive; for example, if someone asks you to get something for them but you don't because you don't agree with his or her choice. Ego manifests itself in many ways. And even when you try not to let your ego step in, it will. Don't beat yourself up over it.

Ultimately, it's not that you have an ego that is a problem. Not paying attention to it, as well as allowing your ego to become your beliefs is where the problem begins. Ego is also apparent when you begin to think less of someone because his or her opinion is different than yours. If you feel that begin to occur, the first thing to do is to stop and remember not to judge. Remind yourself that we each have our own paths and lessons to learn. It is not your place to push your opinions on others.

To do this, you must practice self-awareness. Being aware of your beliefs, your pet peeves and your quirks allows you to identify topics or situations that could cause your ego to react. Self-awareness prepares you, at least most of the time, to catch yourself if you begin to become critical and judgmental of people's life choices.

Self-awareness is particularly important as you become more intuitive. If you are not self-aware, you may mistake your feelings with guidance from the universe. For example, as a teacher I open myself up for messages from students. As a result, more than one student has approached me with what is believed to be spiritual insight. Eight times out of ten, however, the message is an opinion they have formed after hearing something I said in class. Now, the students honestly believe this insight is from the universe, and they are coming from a good place, but it is their opinion. The key to overcoming ego is recognizing the difference. These students were still working on it. They will be working on it for the rest of their lives; we all are.

How do we work on it? How can you tell when your ego and opinions are stepping in, as opposed to it being universal guidance? If not, there is one simple question you can ask yourself. Do the actions of "x" – a person, situation, event – impact me? If it doesn't, it doesn't matter. Let it go. There are too many things in life to address; you don't need clutter.

If it does matter or it continues to bother you, take time for self-reflection. During this reflection, ask yourself some prodding questions, such as, "Why does this bother me?" and "What does this situation remind me of?" Awareness of your opinions and where these opinions came from can help you overcome your ego.

Sometimes it will be easy to identify how a feeling was formed and accept that others may have different opinions. Unfortunately, there are many more beliefs that you likely don't even know you hold. These are the attitudes and beliefs that your parents, grandparents, friends, and society instill in you. These beliefs are hard to overcome. Fortunately, it is not impossible.

Let's go back to the example of my ego with my preference towards cause and effect. Looking at my family history, my father was an accountant and my mother was a nurse. Both fields stressed hard facts and outcomes. Behavioral psychology, more than talk therapy, promised outcomes I could control. Not only that, education and hard work were stressed in my family. Both my parents were college educated. From a young age, I was taught that with hard work anything is possible. That was true of my educational studies. That was also true after my car accident. Hard work made me better. These beliefs where reinforced time and time again.

With my own personal reflection, I have learned that my ego steps in when individuals don't take personal responsibility. Let's take Janis. She has a chronic medical condition that is ill-managed. One of the reasons it is ill-managed is that Janis is a non-compliant patient. She has chosen not to take the recommendations of doctors. She has chosen not to attend therapy. She has chosen not to do the work but rather allow the illness to ravage her body. This used to drive me bonkers! I would get frustrated, even angry, thinking about it. But you know what? Her health status is her choice. If she wanted to change it she could. When I identified my underlying ego, accepting her choice has been easier.

Let's take a moment and identify some of the places your ego may be affecting you.

Exercise 9
Identifying Your Ego

Get a sheet of paper. Sit back and reflect on what is going on in your life currently. Think about your work, family, friends, home, car. As you are doing that, think back over the last twenty-four to seventy-two hours. Identify a situation that has caused you frustration. This situation may have been a minor inconvenience, such as an individual cutting you off to get in the grocery line ahead of you, or it could be one that caused you great anger, such as a colleague lying to you. Big or little, it doesn't matter.

Once you have settled on a situation, ask yourself the following questions:
1) *How did this situation make you feel?* Consider the emotions beyond frustration. If you struggle with identifying emotions, see Appendix A.
2) *Why do you feel these emotions?* For example, if you were cut off in traffic and you are angry, are you mad because you are scared for your safety? Reflect on the situation and identify the root cause of the emotion. Also consider your life theme. How does your archetype respond in these situations?

> 3) *When have you felt this way before?* Continuing the example of being cut off in traffic, perhaps you are sensitive because you were in a severe car accident. Reflect on situations that have elicited this feeling before.
> 4) *How do other people around you behave in similar situations?* We are a social species with a tendency to adopt behaviors of those around us. If your father had a tendency towards road rage, you may have unwittingly adopted the behavior.
> 5) *Any other factors?* Finally, allow yourself to explore other factors that may be influencing your opinions and behaviors, both the obvious and the subtle.
>
> Repeat this exercise as frustrations occur. You will find you have greater insight regarding yourself. You will also find that the frustration you do experience is more moderate.

The self-awareness obtained through the exploration of your ego facilitates improved interactions with your peers as you find yourself more understanding and less argumentative. Additionally, awareness of your ego makes listening to your intuition easier. As you will come to recognize, you are not always right. You don't have all the answers nor is your way always the right or only way. For example, just because you want towels folded one way because they fit "best" in the cabinet doesn't mean that it is the only way to fold the towels or that the towels even need to be placed in the selected cabinet.

ONE

If you are getting anxious from the thought of it, you are not alone. Putting the ego on the shelf is hard and, at times, uncomfortable. Since you will be perfecting this throughout your lifetime, start small. A great place to start is with strangers or people you don't know well. Why? Because you have little or no personal investment in their lives.

The lack of personal investment in my clients' lives is what makes it is easy for me to read them, but not my friends and family. The only investment I have in my client is the desire to be as accurate as possible. Not knowing all the details of their lives, I know I can't begin to understand where they have come from nor can I guess as to what is best for them. My opinions don't matter. Knowing that, I can be objective. Same goes for you. Practicing objectivity and putting the ego to the side is easiest with people you don't know.

Here are a few ways to work through your ego, expectations and judgment. Remember, practice this with strangers and acquaintances first. Only after you are "comfortable" with putting the ego aside for acquaintances, work towards doing so with your friends and family.

First, put yourself in their shoes. Once there, walk yourself through the previous exercise. Looking at the world from the vantage point of someone else is eye opening. One word of caution, don't assume the assumptions you make during this exercise are accurate. You are likely close, but it is unlikely you are one hundred percent accurate. If you assume you are and adopt these assumptions as fact, it will result in misunderstandings. That I can promise you. Once you have viewed the world through someone else's eyes, reflect on your own life. How can you make his or her life better? What can you do to be more understanding? Adjust your behavior accordingly. Finally, provide any words of insight, but be objective. Listen to your heart and your intuition. By practicing this, you will likely become the person people turn to for advice.

While you become the go-to for good advice for other people, you may still struggle to find that same wisdom for yourself. The reason is simple. You are not, and never will be, objective when it comes to your life. You want certain things. You may want to date a particular person. You may desire a certain car or to live in a specific area. Or it may be that in an argument, you just want to be right. Whatever it is, you are not a blank slate. You have your point of view. Your point of view is the lens through which all your intuition is filtered. Passing through this filter, you will likely interpret messages in a way that affirms the direction you wish to be going. In addition, you will assume your intuition is supporting actions that you believe will move you towards your desires.

Let's explore another example to see how we can interpret messages in a manner we desire. A few years ago I took a position that required relocation. In retrospect, the universe was encouraging me not to take the position. The hiring process was dragged out. I knew the relocation would have a negative impact on my business, and the offer was less than the amount my husband and I decided was the bare minimum. Still, within days of my accepting the job, I found a beautiful penthouse apartment within walking distance of work, it allowed for dogs and it gave me a break on rent. At the time, I interpreted the ease with which housing fell into place as a sign that the decision I made was correct. In reality, the universe was just helping a girl out.

ONE

A lesson that can be learned from this is, if you continue to ask for additional signs, eventually one will come that supports your wants and desires. It is like Lynn. She presented her primary care doctor with a set of symptoms that caused him believe the symptoms could be indicative of fibromyalgia. After running a series of tests and meeting with a specialist, it was the specialist's opinion her physician was incorrect in his assessment. She did not have fibromyalgia. Disappointed, she saw eight more doctors. The ninth was the first to agree with her doctor's diagnosis and diagnosed her with fibromyalgia. She sought the answer, and eventually she got it. The same thing is true for an individual asking the universe. If you keep asking, eventually you will get the answer you desire.

You might be thinking, "How do I avoid this pitfall?" or "How do I know it's my ego and not my intuition?" If you are asking either of these questions, it is likely your ego is influencing your interpretation of the signs the universe is providing you in some way. Being aware of that is a good sign. Awareness is the first step to counteracting the effects of ego. The next step is asking yourself the following questions:

1) *How badly do I want to believe what my "intuition" is telling me?* If the signs appear to be pointing towards something you crave and desire, then you want to be cautious.
2) *Is the advice I am giving myself the same advice I would give to a stranger?* Consider all the information you have at your fingertips and imagine a stranger is telling you the story. If you wouldn't be giving that stranger the same advice, you want to reconsider following it yourself.

3) *Is the situation progressing in a positive manner?* This question is only suitable if you have begun following the advice. If you have taken steps and the situation is going poorly, stop immediately and reevaluate. You very well may be driven by ego, not intuition.

Let's look at an example in which asking these questions could have been beneficial. Kendra, a talented and aspiring medium, was desperate to leave her day job to become a professional medium. She meditated and received confirmation that mediumship was part of her path. Dedicated to changing careers, she took class after class, read everything she could get her hands on and formed plans for an office where she could see clients.

Despite her dedication, Kendra's plans were continuously interrupted. Sometimes it was her husband. He didn't understand or support her desire and wanted her to spend more time with the family. Other times it was work. Her clients were making her jump through hoops and colleagues were creating a toxic work environment. Yet she still felt divinely guided. More than that, Kendra wanted more than anything to be a professional medium. Stubbornly, she continued towards her goal. That stubbornness and haste resulted in the loss of her marriage and many of her longstanding clients, which ultimately decreased her revenue. Not only that, she is no further towards her goal of becoming a professional medium. Had she asked the questions above, Kendra might have recognized the universe was telling her to slow down.

She was following her intuition but was fighting an uphill battle. It would have behooved her to slow down and reevaluate. If you find yourself in a similar situation, that is what I encourage you to do. Stop. Ask. Why are you doing what you are? Is it because it "feels" right? Or is it because it is what you want? If it is what you want, why? Perhaps there is a "better" solution than the one at hand. How will you find out? Listen. What you may find is that it isn't right for you. Or perhaps, timing is off. Sometimes, it is the right thing but not the right time.

Timing is important and everything in life happens in its time and its place. Just as you can't make water boil faster, you can't learn life lessons any faster, which presents another challenge for the ego. The ego doesn't like the waiting game. It wants to plan. It wants situations to fall into place, and fast. Unfortunately, life doesn't work that way. Think about the impactful moments and decisions of your life. Were they the ones you forced? Ones you planned for? Or were they the ones that just seemed to happen? Chances are they just seemed to fall into place.

For example, while exploring my intuition and finishing my degree, I was coasting. I didn't have a steady job, nor was I looking for one. I was waiting to see what happened, but while at a retreat, I hit it off with one of the other women. One conversation flowed into another, and at some point (I don't even remember how the conversation took this turn) she asked, "Are you looking for a job? I'm looking for an administrative assistant. Send me your resume." Soon as I got home, I did.

That simple exchange changed my life. I started as a consultant doing little bits of administrative work here and there. I was then brought on as a full-time assistant. As the organization grew, so did I. I became a coordinator and left the organization as a director. Wearing many hats throughout the years, I gained many skills, all of which I use in my business today.

The relationship between us couldn't have been forced. And had I looked for the job, I wouldn't have found it. At the time, it wasn't posted anywhere. Just like that, nothing in life can be forced. It is sort of like when you pick a tomato that is still green. It might become red when off the vine, but it will never be as sweet as if it were left to ripen. In life that occurs time and time again. We want things to happen sooner, but sometimes we must wait.

This was apparent in the following situation with a close friend of mine. Justin wanted love very badly. He worked hard to communicate with the universe so he could be better directed towards that love. Despite getting the signs that love was right around the corner, the relationship didn't come, until he met someone that was everything he desired. As he and this person got to know each other, he realized that had he met her six months earlier the relationship would not have been. Six months prior, they were both in places that would not have facilitated the relationship, most notably she was still in a relationship. The timing was off then.

The same will be true for you. You will find there are times your ego really wants something, but you have a nagging feeling it isn't right for you. The nagging feeling, or intuition, will be subtle and you, as mentioned earlier, have your perception. With your filter, you could easily choose to interpret the messages to fit what you want to hear or continue to ask the same question until you receive the answer you desire. In the end, however, you will know you are lying to yourself. And you know what? The universe will let you lie to yourself. It is your life after all. Only on rare occasions does the universe force a decision or action upon you. Working with the universe, checking, negotiating and making compromises will make this process smoother.

ONE

This was the case when it came to my husband. The universe had determined it was time for me to have a significant other. From what I could gather, it felt that I could no longer "do what I needed to do" alone. I didn't understand this sentiment at the time as I felt I was doing just fine. When I observed couples, all I saw was bitterness, unhappiness and sacrifice. Why would I want that? Yet the universe persisted. Everywhere I turned a new potential suitor popped up. Displeased with the options and exhausted by the insistence that it "knew" better than I did, I decided to heed the signs and "see" what was out there, but I also made it clear it would be on my terms. In an effort to be clear as to what my terms were, I sat down and made a list. After thinking long and hard about the situation, I narrowed it down to ten items I deemed most important in a partner. Some of them were foolish. For example, I wanted someone to sing to me. I regret every day I forgot to add the qualifier "well." Some were incredibly important, such as he needed to support me in my business.

Well, I cannot say the universe never works for me because it brought me my husband in a spectacular fashion. And he proved to be everything on my list. And a deal is a deal. The universe worked on my terms; I couldn't back out of my end of the deal. Here we are, still together. And you know what, the universe was right. I did need him. Without him, I wouldn't be where I am personally or professionally. Had I used the Identifying Ego exercise at the time, I would have realized part of my hesitancy with a new relationship had to do with my parents. I love both my parents as individuals tremendously. But as a couple, they weren't a good fit. Upon reflection, I realized that my independence and desire to do it alone are a result of witnessing my parents' dissatisfaction in their relationship. They needed to account for the other's needs and didn't necessarily feel as though their needs were accounted for. This was something I saw, a dissatisfaction I felt. And it was something I decided I wanted to avoid. I didn't want a partner because I didn't know what a partner was, but, I listened to the universe, and I'm glad I did.

As in the situation with my husband, when you listen you may be compelled to do something you don't want to or that seems to be against your best interest. For example, my husband and I had planned a trip down to see his family. It had been over a year since we had visited and his family had seen our daughter. Intuitively, I had a nagging feeling that we shouldn't go. Assuming these feelings were ego, they were dismissed, but the feelings persisted, and then my uncle became ill. Several days later, he was gone. We had to rearrange our calendar.

It would have been nice, and alleviated the concern my ego was experiencing, had the universe provided details regarding the nagging feeling. Unfortunately, intuition doesn't work that way. And despite reflection, I couldn't force a message. Too many details were involved; and, it takes away from the journey of life. Not only that, too much information might not be for your highest and best or the highest and best for the world. For example, wouldn't it be great if we had the ability to intuit the lottery numbers? If that were possible, how might my life change? How much of my life's purpose would be thrown off track?

That doesn't mean that the universe can't provide the lottery numbers. In fact, Colette shared that she did receive the winning lottery numbers from the universe. It was just after her son was born. Colette wasn't working and her husband's job was in flux. The small but sizable winnings were enough to tide them over. It was for their highest and best in the moment.

The universe provides all the time. So how do you tap into this wisdom? How do you utilize the universe towards reaching your highest potential, not just in times of stress but in good times as well? It starts with identifying the subtle difference between ego and intuition. This is hard, but considering the following question can offer great insight. Do you feel you need to be right? Feeling you need to argue a situation or prove you are right is a clear indication of ego, not intuition. Dost thou protest too much?

Unfortunately, this is something that happens too often, especially in students of mediumship. Let's consider Rose, a practicing Tarot student who read the cards for my husband. Familiar with various aspects of his life, upon looking at the cards in front of her, she made an assumption and ran with it. Because he is open-minded, he understood the broad meaning despite her incorrect details. When he tried to steer her in a different direction, she simply stated, "No. You are wrong. That's not what it means. It means this." Rose was unwilling to see any other potential, and in the end, she was wrong. What she insisted never came to pass… but what my husband felt would, did.

This is an example of how one's assumptions and ego can be placed on another. We do this to ourselves as well. We jinx or trick ourselves into believing something is true when it really isn't. A good example of this is when my husband and I were buying our house. We had a list of must-haves. We then identified the area we wanted to live in and were open to finding a place. We'd looked at about two dozen houses but couldn't find the perfect house.

My husband was getting frustrated with the process and really wanted to find our forever home. It was then that our realtor showed us a cute blue and white house. It was a lovely house in the area we wanted to be in. Walking into the home, my husband was sold. I was not. While it was cute, and was better than a lot of places we'd walked into, it lacked many of our must-haves. It didn't have a room in which I could do readings. The kitchen was galley-style and if one person were in there, another couldn't walk by. It needed a new roof. It was within our price range but higher than we wanted to spend.

After seeing it, I was ready to move on to the next. My husband was not. A few days later, after much discussion, we called our realtor and asked that he arrange a second viewing. It was a hassle to get in. It should have been a sign, but we went anyway. During the second viewing, I had the same concerns. Despite the concerns, my husband insisted we make an offer on the house. We waited. And waited. And when the homeowner's realtor finally came back with a counter, we found out that the property was already in contract. In fact, the house had been in contract since before we saw the house the first time. My husband was devastated. He had convinced himself that it was our forever home. He imagined signs that seemed to support the fact it was supposed to be our home, but it wasn't. Ours ended up being around the corner.

It is important to remind yourself that if you have to convince yourself something is true, it probably isn't. More likely, it is your ego talking. Intuition either is or it isn't. There is no need to ponder it.

ONE

CHAPTER 12
RESPECT

"Having respect for the world is when you allow people to be what they are."
Magda Gerber

Recognition of ego is one thing, but keeping it in line is another. An ongoing practice of humility is necessary if you hope to keep your ego in check. To be humble, you must practice both Respect and Gratitude. In this chapter, we will talk about Respect.

Individuals who use their intuition are often open-minded and see the world from a different vantage point than their less intuitive peers. While new to intuition, you will experience joy, peace and a sense of belonging that you have not felt before. Excited about this new experience, you will want to share your experience with everyone. Being preoccupied and excited about the insights you've recently received will become the topic of conversation at breakfast, in the break room at work, over drinks and before bed. Filled with joy, it is not uncommon for you to want your friends, family and acquaintances to have the same experience. As a result, you may attempt to replicate and demonstrate the insights you've had, or you may encourage your loved ones to attend the workshop or read the book you did. This is where a problem can occur and practicing respect is critical.

Despite how wonderful you feel, not everyone in your life may be comfortable with expanding their intuition. Your loved ones may not want to discuss the topic of spirituality, hear about the workshop you attended or read the book you read. In fact, they may look at you like you are bonkers, encourage you to stop your journey and hope that things will go back to the way they used to be. Why? Your loved ones may have the fears discussed in Chapter 7 or the spirituality you have found may just not be their "thing."

Let's use a food metaphor to explore this further. The intuitive, you, is like a person who has just found an amazing eggplant parmesan recipe. You find this recipe so tasty that you want to make it for your family. One of your family members, however, doesn't like eggplant. And despite how good you think it is, they are not wowed by this new recipe. They may not even want to take a bite. You can't change their food preferences. It would be silly to try. Similarly, as you awaken and become more intuitive, you must be respectful of others and recognize that each person has his or her own set of desires, truths and lessons to learn. They may not want to use their intuition. It might seem crazy to you, but not everyone does.

Caught up in the good vibes you are feeling while using your intuition, you may not understand why an individual would choose not to become awakened. It will be, as it often is, your perception that life is better with intuition than without. This inability to understand is where the ego begins to step in and judgement begins to be cast.

If you feel that happening. Here are some things to remember. First, being intuitive is not better than not being intuitive. It's like choosing a religion. Buddhism is not better than Christianity, which is not better than Hinduism or even Atheism. They are just different.

Secondly, it has been my experience that people new to their intuition use the Identifying Ego exercise discussed in the last chapter incorrectly. You may have been one of those people. This is nothing to be ashamed of; it happens, but if used incorrectly, the ego seizes the opportunity to step in. How do intuitives use the Identifying Ego exercise incorrectly? They feel like they have overcome any or all obstacles by being more open-minded, intuitive or enlightened. With this they assume "Awakened or Intuitive is Best." They then see the world through this lens. As a result, any challenges they believe their loved ones are facing they assume can be overcome through intuition and becoming more spiritual. However, this is not always the case. The challenges you assume your loved one is having may not be perceived as a problem at all. In fact, that loved one may be exactly where he or she wants and even needs to be.

By butting in to "aid" your "less" intuitive loved ones with unsolicited advice, you may be hurting or annoying them. They may feel judged and hurt and may not be receptive to the advice given. If offended, they may blame your newly found spirituality. If they do take your advice, it may lead to more problems because it is not what they needed to hear.

If you offer unsolicited advice, chances are you will find yourself frustrated. This frustration could be because you feel your loved ones aren't listening; you might feel judged; or, you might believe they didn't follow your advice properly. Whatever it may be, you are likely going

RESPECT

to try harder to get them to listen, which may result in preaching. Preaching is the ego, which will without a doubt aggravate the person you are trying to assist. And I'm sure you can see where this cycle leads.

While both individuals play a role in this cycle, if you want your intuition to continue to thrive, if a situation like this occurs, you need to accept your responsibility for the situation, especially if you hit the "preaching stage." Don't blame your loved one. Look at your own behavior. At this point you may be righteous, assuming the "messages" being received are from intuition and what is "right" for your peer. What is more likely is that you are touting your newly formed beliefs, not intuition, nor what is right for the peer.

How can you avoid this? While you are encouraged to make observations and draw conclusions from your observations, as this insight can help you navigate situations, don't believe your assumptions are one hundred percent accurate. Don't stop observing once you make your conclusions. Don't become so wedded to the conclusions that you can't perceive anything else could be possible. Additionally, don't stop honing those conclusions. They will change. You cannot possibly know everything. You are not God.

Had my husband used this advice, he could have avoided heartache. Let's look at this example. As spring was approaching and our daughter was growing, he thought a great activity for family time would be riding bikes. There was a problem however. Due to my limited eyesight and trouble with balance, I can't ride a bike. To solve the problems, he researched various options and found a tricycle that he thought was a great solution. When he presented it to me, I responded with disinterest. He proceeded to try to convince me this was the perfect solution. What he didn't take into account was that biking wasn't my thing. As a result, I didn't see not biking as a problem. Just as in this situation, you may perceive a problem that doesn't exist because others' perceptions are different than your own. By not believing those perceptions, it makes it easier to let them go.

Along with not making assumptions, don't assume individuals are less intuitive or spiritual just because they don't practice the same way you do. Intuition doesn't manifest itself in the same ways. Someone can be gruff and rough around the edges and still be enlightened. In fact, some of the most spiritual and intuitive people I know wouldn't call themselves intuitive. It is important to remember that intuition has a lot to do with being a good person, and appearance doesn't always denote that.

As mentioned, making assumptions is an obstacle that occurs in all individuals. You will not be immune. If you think you are, reread the last chapter and observe your situations a little more closely, especially in your closest relationships. And if you are married, pay close attention there. Every student I have ever had, at one time for another, indicates problems in their marriage as they evolve, even when they are attending classes together. Why? All persons grow at their own rate. As a result, some people are bound to evolve at a pace quicker than their partner, if their partner is evolving at all.

Why does this cause problems? Intuitives want to share their new experiences with their partners and loved ones. As mentioned, we all evolve at our own rate. Besides, people do not experience intuition or spirituality in the same way. The journey is unique and individual. So even when they are supportive of one another and are growing together, they are also growing apart. As a result, they end up frustrated that they feel like they are doing it alone.

This was the case with Cameron and Felicia, a couple who came to classes hoping to grow their intuition. The conscientious couple was aware that each had unique gifts and would thrive at different rates. And that was the case. Cameron jumped in and thrived right away. He was a sponge for knowledge; additionally, he took everything he learned and immediately applied it to his everyday life. He was practicing protection, talking to guides and deceased loved ones, even trying his hand at manifesting. Nothing was off limits.

This posed a problem for Felicia. She was a natural intuitive who wanted nothing more than to learn how to shut her intuition off when necessary. Unfortunately, Felicia found the more intuitive Cameron became, the more disrupted her life became. She had trouble sleeping and experienced migraines. Her career was even affected as her clients and colleagues would congregate in her office just to be near her. The lack of sleep, the constant physical discomfort and the pull from those around her were leaving her drained.

This struggle began affecting their marriage. Both wanted to support the other, but Cameron's growth was affecting her health and by hindering his growth Felicia was affecting his purpose. The result was that both were inadvertently affecting the other. Fortunately, the two were able to respect each other's needs and desires. After talking and working through their assumptions, they found a balance that worked for both of them.

Finding that balance and respecting those individuals and the place they are in is of utmost importance. While doing this, trust that you each have a role to play in the other's life. Trust that those differences of opinion will make you better. The key, however, is to understand or at least hear those differences. Once you hear them, don't be offended if they don't see your point of view, and remember it may not be theirs to see. For example, my husband has an interest in exploring shamanism. I, on the other hand, have no interest in reading books or learning about that form of healing. It can be part of his journey and not mine.

The same goes for you and the people around you. For example, teaching may be part of someone else's path and not yours. That is okay! It is what makes the world so interesting. If we were all the same, it would be a boring place to live. The important aspect of that, however, is that even though it is not part of your journey, you respect their path. You may not understand why. It may not resonate with you. You might not even know anything about it, but it is important to respect it nonetheless.

Lack of respect for other's belief systems is what leads to prejudice and religious wars. This happens in both global and one-on-one situations. On the global level, lack of respect due to a lack of understanding was apparent in pre-WWII Germany and post-9/11 United States. In Germany it was the persecution of Jews, whereas in the United States there was a fear of Muslims. Many spiritual people dismiss this as, "I'm not that person." But perhaps you are.

Have you ever attended a gathering and heard someone talk about a topic such as aliens or time travel, and thought to yourself, "That individual is nuts!" In that instance, you made a judgment. By dismissing them, you have dismissed their truth and while their truth might not be what you believe, that doesn't mean that it is any less true.

Let's explore this thought in terms of religion. Let's assume you are Christian. As a Christian, you believe in God. Your belief is that God sent Jesus here to repent for our sins. You pray to him and perhaps the Saints. And you turn to the Bible for your teachings. Should you accept these teachings, you believe there will be a place for you after death in heaven. Recently, you have become acquainted with a Hindu. Respecting him, you have learned a little about his religion and found that rather than turning to the Bible, he turns to the Vedas. You can accept that, as it is his religious text. You can also accept his belief that he will find his place with Brahman, his God, after his death. This is where it begins to get odd for you. He will only find his place with Brahman (heaven) after he reaches dharma, which is accomplished through reincarnation. You aren't sure you believe in that. Nor are you comfortable with him praying to the unfamiliar Hindu gods and goddesses, such as Vishnu and Lakshmi.

A hesitancy to accept another's beliefs demonstrates lack of respect. This lack of respect makes it hard for the universe to communicate with you and assist you in personal growth as it limits where you can grow to. If you do not allow yourself to go outside your comfort zone, you can only go so far.

ONE

CHAPTER 13
GRATITUDE

"As we express our gratitude, we must never forget that the highest appreciation is not to utter words, but to live by them."
John F Kennedy

With respect comes the practice of gratitude. Are you feeling proud of yourself for the growth you've had? Are you giving yourself pats on the back for how intuitive you are? You should. It is a lot of work and it can be a struggle to grow spirituality, but have you also said thank you to the universe? If you haven't, you should. Why? Because by now you should realize that your intuition is much larger than you. Your intuition is not a result of how wise you have become. Nor is it solely indicative of how much work and effort you have put in. The universe has played a big part in your evolution. The universe has organized synchronicities. It has given you signs for the purpose of directing you towards your life purpose. Not only that, the universe assisted in opening your mind to accept the change and evolution occurring within you. For all that, it deserves gratitude.

GRATITUDE

If that hasn't convinced you, go back and reread Chapter 9. In that chapter, your soul and life purposes were discussed. It should have been evident that your role here on Earth is bigger than just you. Once you recognize that, life becomes easier. The same thing occurs with gratitude. Recognizing the role the universe plays makes it work harder and your life easier. It is then that magic happens.

Let's liken this to a child who has drawn you a picture. If you express gratitude by exclaiming how beautiful it is, pointing out how creative the child is and promise to hang the picture on the refrigerator, chances are you are going to get another drawing from that child. Also, that next picture will likely be more elaborate. The child, filled with joy, wants to share that happiness with you. The same is true of the universe. When acknowledged and appreciated, the universe will go out of its way to bring joy into your life.

This occurred when my husband and I took our daughter to Disney. We had read blog after blog on how to get the most out of Disney with a toddler. In preparation, we determined the one "must do" while there. We then ranked other attractions in terms of importance should we have time. With that in mind, we scheduled our Fast-Passes and planned our day. We'd done our part, now the universe stepped in. First, my step-brother provided us with additional fast-passes which gave us the ability to hop on other rides more quickly. Thanking the universe, they then kicked it up another notch. As we walked around the park, we always seemed to be in the right place at the right time. We would bump into the characters and were literally able to walk right up and get a photo. Additionally, the universe provided us with several impromptu photo ops where the Disney

ONE

photographers snapped photos of our family. The synchronicities were abundant. It was a beautiful day provided to us with the help of the universe. And the more gratitude we expressed, the more we got out of the day.

It's important to note that you don't have to be ridiculous with gratitude. All the universe needs is a little acknowledgment. If you are over the top, the gratitude can become ingenuine, which is counterproductive, especially since acknowledgement of the universe's role is more for you than it. When you forget that intuition is a partnership, it is only a matter of time before the ego steps back in and you begin to take all the credit. Should this happen, you may become arrogant. The universe's signs may become muted as you begin to insert your own thoughts and opinions into the messages you are receiving. Should that happen, your intuition becomes corrupted and people could get hurt, both you and the people around you.

This regression is a tragedy to witness. A person not only stops growing but also regresses. Unfortunately, I have witnessed this in quite a few people. One case I'll share with you is Amy, a student that had trained with me for several years. When she first started coming, she developed at a rapid pace. She was open-minded and embraced what the universe could provide with open arms. Because she did, she witnessed synchronicities all around her and would often find herself in the right place at the right time. For example, one day she bumped into an old friend who just so happened to be able to provide insight and direct her as to how to launch her intuitive business. Amy felt blessed and honored to have this new skill and the universe on her side.

Then Amy began to change. It was small at first. She began crediting herself for the insights she had, forgetting the role of the universe. She'd do this when describing the synchronicities in her life. I overheard her saying on more than one occasion, "I'm not saying it was me, but I asked and…" whatever she had asked for came to pass. She was personalizing the magic as opposed to seeing the universe's role. Not only that, she began making requests of the universe that were not for the highest and best. This is a big no-no when you are approaching the world with love and light. For example, I heard her state that she hoped the karma her boss had coming to him would be sped up. I cringed when she told me the story, but I took a deep breath and reminded myself this was her path. Amy hadn't at any time during the story asked for my opinion. Keeping my ego in check and practicing respect, I kept my mouth shut.

Amy continued to change. As she did, I started paying closer attention to her readings. In doing so, I realized the messages she was providing other students were less accurate and more negative. Classmates noticed it as well, and they confided that they hoped they were not paired up with her in class. Attempting to turn this tide, during the critique portion of practice, I asked questions similar to those provided in the Ego Chapter with the hope that it would open her eyes. Unfortunately, rather than becoming more reflective, she would respond with statements like, "I feel" and "It might not make sense now, but hold on to it." When those phrases cross a person's lips, I don't push further as it becomes obvious the individual is not interested in assistance. At that point it is not my place to offer it. This was the case with Amy.

Why didn't Amy want my assistance? Because she no longer sees herself as the student. What she fails to realize is there are always going to be lessons to be learned. It might be limited to a phrase or a small nugget,

ONE

but there is always a takeaway. So even though she considers her evolution to have made us peers, truth is we were always equals and at the same time we will never be equals. As long as I am in her life, she will have lessons to learn from me, but at the same time I have lessons to learn from her. My students are one of my greatest blessings and as a teacher, I am constantly learning from them. Because of the lack of gratitude to the universe, Amy's ego has reared up. She has forgotten this.

Amy might not be asking the universe's assistance as much right now and is instead turning to her own wisdom; that doesn't mean the universe has forsaken her. The universe stays by her side, continuing to support her by providing signs and direction. Once she gets her ego in check, her spiritual growth will return. To do that, she first needs to recognize her ego is running the show. Then she needs to practice respect and gratitude. In that gratitude, apologies may be given to those she has hurt along the way, which would include herself.

It's important that gratitude is genuine and not just lip service. When rendering gratitude as part of lip service, you aren't fooling the universe. The only one you might be fooling is yourself. False gratitude is just one way of feeding the ego.

Let me use Tony as an example. He is a client of a friend of mine. For my friend, Tony is the nightmare client. Tony considers himself to be a spiritual individual and recognizes the importance of gratitude. Knowing its importance, he will express gratitude to my friend's face. Tony will thank my friend for working late into the night. Thank her for being available at the drop of a hat. Thank her for her insight and expertise. But he will then at the slightest frustration make snide comments that question her expertise despite Tony's minimal comprehension of the subject matter. Tony also becomes argumentative and passive aggressive throughout the working arrangement. He never outright disagrees, but the tone says it all. His actions speak louder than his words. Why is Tony acting this way? He has certain expectations about how the process should go that are not being met.

Situations like this may happen while you are working with the universe. You may have a certain expectation about what should happen, how long it should take, where you should be or how you should feel; and then it doesn't happen. You will be disappointed. The universe doesn't always provide you with what you want. Rather than expressing false gratitude like Tony did, express your frustration. Let the universe hear your disappointment. By doing so, you give the universe a sense of not only what isn't working but also what you want. Knowing this, it can work harder to help you get what you want. This leads to trust.

You are encouraged to express your frustration. Once you have, however, let it go. Work hard to find the good in the situation. If you can't, find something, anything good in your life and express gratitude for that. Why? By expressing gratitude in times of turmoil, it opens the doorway for new beginnings. It brings hope. With hope, you can see opportunities, whereas if you remain frustrated and perhaps pessimistic, you are more likely to miss the opportunities presented.

For example, a few years ago I quit a job because I was 98% certain I had another job lined up. I'd interviewed for the job with the Executive Director. At the time, she all but promised me the position. When she informed me that I would have to interview the Board Chair, she assured me this was protocol and that I had nothing to worry about. Turns out, I should have worried.

ONE

I didn't get the position. I was really frustrated when the Executive Director gave me the reason the other candidate was selected over myself. Apparently, the Board Chair felt I lacked experience in a portion of the job description. The frustrating part about that was neither the Board Chair or Executive Director had asked me any questions regarding those duties. Had they, I would have outlined my extensive experience in that area. At the time I was furious, but after a day or so, I resigned myself to believe the universe had something greater in mind for me. Knowing the universe would provide, I offered my gratitude to it for helping point me in the right direction, and it did. I love my life. It would be completely different if I had taken the position. The universe knew better than I did.

With all this talk about gratitude, you are probably asking: How do I express gratitude? Here are some tips on ways to express gratitude:

1) *Thank You!* – How often, after circumstances fall into place, do you say thank you? For example, your kids need to be picked up from daycare at 3:00 pm. You have gotten stuck in a meeting and you are unable to get ahold of your husband. Upon calling the school, they tell you they are unable to keep your kids beyond 3:30 pm. Struggling to figure it out, you get a phone call from a mom from the daycare and she tells you, "Don't worry about it. I've got you covered!" Did you say thank you to her? Probably. To the daycare workers who helped arrange it? Again, probably. But did you offer gratitude to the universe? Maybe, maybe not. If you didn't, you should. It is circumstances like that where it is helping you. The more you thank the universe, the more it wants to help you out.

2) *Find the Silver Lining* – Do you look at the glass as half empty or half full? Many intuitives would say, neither. They are grateful to have the cup that they can keep filling. By finding the opportunities, you are seeing how the universe is lining things up. Miracles don't happen overnight. Many things take time.
3) *Practice Humility* – As discussed earlier in the chapter, it is important that you remember you are just one small part of a greater whole.
4) *Go the Extra Mile* – Be generous with your resources, be it through time, money, advice or something else. For me this equates to frequently going over the allotted amount of time in a reading. I keep this within reason, but when my buzzer goes off I'm not kicking the client out the door. This goes a long way. Think of your doctor: are you going to have a greater affinity and faith in your physician if he is sitting listening to your concerns or if he has one hand on the door, rushing you? The answer is evident. By giving of yourself, it demonstrates your gratitude to the universe.
5) *Random Acts of Kindness* – Being generous should not be limited to those in your inner circle, but also for those you may never see again. Be generous just because.
6) *Be Genuine* – Don't have ulterior motives and do things for the "positive karma." When I would work the psychic fairs, there was one reader who, whenever she was having a slow weekend, would walk around the show and purchase items from the vendors, not because she was drawn to the goods but because she believed that if she spent money she would get money in return. From what

ONE

I could tell, it didn't work. Actions taken just to get you ahead often set you further behind.

Using these tips everyday will keep your intuition pure and will keep the universe working for you at a super-charged rate.

CHAPTER 14
PATIENCE

"Have patience with all things, but first of all with yourself."
Saint Francis de Sales

The process of perceiving, trusting and utilizing your intuition is not easy. It does not happen overnight. With that in mind, it is important for you to have patience. Be patient with the universe, but more importantly, be patient with yourself.

A great example of patience is Joy. She was dedicated to developing her intuition and she attended session after session. She would eagerly participate in each exercise, but at the end of each class Joy would smile but disappointedly exclaim, "Still nothing" as her intuition had not spoken to her. The lack of connection with the universe went on not just for months, but years. Yet, she persisted. And after a few years, something clicked and the intuition flowed.

Why did it take so long for Joy's intuition to kick into gear? Perhaps she wasn't ready. Perhaps she still had lessons to learn. There are lots of reasons one could consider, many more that one cannot, for why her intuition was blocked. Joy exercised extraordinary patience and it paid off. Many, perhaps even you, would have given up, but as the saying goes, "Anything worth having is worth the wait." And with intuition, I can promise you it is.

I know patience is hard, especially in the fast-paced society within which we live. We aren't accustomed to having to wait. Think about it for a moment. Do you get frustrated when the shipping of the item you ordered online is delayed? Or when the food you ordered takes a little longer than normal? Most likely. That is the way of our world.

To help you practice patience on your journey to intuition, here are some tips:

1) *Limit the Time You Practice* – The journey to awareness is exciting. It is likely you are going to want to practice and engage in spiritual activities all the time. You will force yourself to meditate. You will find yourself only attending spiritual classes, watching spiritual movies and engaging in spiritual conversations. Even though that's what you will want to do, I encourage you not to. Just like the athlete who needs to rest his muscles, you too need to rest. Intuition is a muscle. If you push it too hard and don't give it time to rest, you will likely experience setbacks.

2) *Keep Other Interests* – We are spiritual beings having a physical existence. If we were only meant to have spiritual experiences, we wouldn't have a physical body and exist on the earthly plane. There is so much to experience here on earth; be certain to take advantage of it. If you like to hike, hike. If cooking is your passion, cook. And do it with gusto! If you choose to only focus on your intuition and you hit a plateau, you will find yourself getting frustrated.

PATIENCE

3) *Celebrate the Small Victories* – Intuition doesn't happen overnight. You aren't going to hear the booming voice of God and suddenly be enlightened. Becoming awakened will occur in small steps. At each step, celebrate. When you receive a sign, let out a wahoo!
4) *Breathe Deeply* – If you find yourself becoming frustrated, take a deep breath. This is the simplest and most powerful tool you have in your tool belt. Use it.
5) *Have Fun* – This is the most important one. If awakening becomes work or a chore, you aren't doing it right. Becoming enlightened is about making your life easier, not harder. And ultimately, if you are having fun, you won't have to worry about patience. Every step of the way will be a blast.

ONE

EPILOGUE

"Give the girl the right shoes, and she can conquer the world"
Marilyn Monroe

Well my friends, here we are at the end. You have just finished reading my take on how the energy of intuition works, how the universe communicates with each of us and how you can better receive messages from the universe. Remember, this book only encompasses my take on the subject. It is my truth. My understanding. Through my lens.

Now it's your turn to go out and explore. Using the tools provided throughout this book, you are encouraged to go find your truth, your understanding of the world and your place in it. Do this by exploring. Read everything you can get your hands on, even if it doesn't interest you. Talk to anyone who will listen, and listen to anyone who wants to share his or her perspective.

While exploring, be curious. Don't be afraid. Raise your hand and ask lots of questions. If a book you have read sparks questions, contact the author. What's the worst that could happen? You don't get a response? But what if you do? If you have a question about a statement someone has made or aren't familiar with a topic they are discussing, ask them about it. These opportunities to interact are invaluable and will provide you with tremendous insight. That insight will only come, however, if you listen. Be sure to listen intently to everything that is being said, by both your fellow man and the universe. Listen with you head for facts. Your heart for feelings. Your spirit for the why. As you listen, practice compassion, respect and gratitude. You don't have to agree, or even like every interaction you have, but be certain to find the blessing each moment brings and be grateful.

Do these things every day. Every single day. Meditate. Write. Sing. Dance. Commune with nature. Look for the signs. By doing these things, you will find the joy in your intuition. You will find the energy that connects us all.

With that, I will end with my expression of gratitude to each of you. Thank you for joining me on this journey. May you find the joy I have. Peace, love and blessings!

APPENDIX A
Positive and Negative Emotions[7]

Below is a list of emotions to assist you in getting in touch with your inner self as well as the universe. This is not a complete list. If you are looking for a more comprehensive list, check out the Center for Nonviolent Communication at www.cnvc.org.

Positive Emotions

Acceptance	Devotion	Inspiration	Relaxation
Admiration	Eagerness	Invigoration	Renewal
Affection	Elation	Joy	Respect
Appreciation	Empowerment	Jubilation	Rested
Astonishment	Encouragement	Love	Safety
Awe	Engagement	Mellowness	Satisfaction
Bliss	Enthusiasm	Motivation	Serenity
Calm	Excitement	Optimism	Success
Compassion	Faith	Passion	Surprise
Confidence	Fulfillment	Peace	Sympathy
Contentment	Giddiness	Playfulness	Tenderness
Courage	Gratefulness	Pleasure	Touched
Creativity	Happiness	Pride	Trust
Curiosity	Hopefulness	Refreshed	Wonder
Delight	Honor	Reflection	Worthiness

ONE

Negative Emotions

Aggravation	Discouragement	Heartbreak	Rage
Agony	Distrust	Helplessness	Regret
Alienation	Dread	Hesitancy	Remorse
Ambivalence	Embarrassment	Hopelessness	Resentment
Anger	Emptiness	Impatience	Restlessness
Annoyance	Envy	Indifference	Sadness
Anxiety	Fatigue	Indignance	Self-Consciousness
Apprehension	Fear	Judgment	Shame
Boredom	Foreboding	Loneliness	Suspicion
Combativeness	Fright	Longing	Terror
Confusion	Frustration	Lost	Unsettlement
Contempt	Gloom	Melancholy	Vulnerability
Depleted	Grief	Pain	Withdrawn
Disappointment	Guilt	Panic	Worn Out
Disconnect	Hate	Overwhelmed	Worry

APPENDIX B
The Twelve Archetypes[8]

The archetypes described below are based on the research of Carol S. Pearson, PhD and CASA: Center for Archetypal Studies and Applications Resources. More detailed information regarding these archetypes is available on her website, www.carolspearson.com.

THE INNOCENT
The Innocent can be likened to the Fool in the Tarot. These individuals are full of optimism for the future. They trust in the universe and have hope. There may be some naivete. They fear abandonment.

THE ORPHAN
The Orphan is also known as the victim. These individuals have suffered at the hand of others. As a result, they expect little and have become resilient and resourceful, trusting only themselves. They fear lack of control and losing what they have worked hard to earn.

THE WARRIOR
The Warrior is the Hero. People associated with this archetype help save the day and helps others achieve their goals. They never give up and rarely compromise, as they see the world in terms of black and white. They fear failure.

THE CAREGIVER
The Caregiver are the Mother and the person people lean on. Those individuals are compassionate and selfless. They help others achieve their dreams. Unfortunately, this sometimes ends up hurting the caregivers.

ONE

THE SEEKER
The Seeker describes those who tend to keep to themselves and walk to the beat of their own drum. They seek a greater understanding of the world and as a result, leave the known to explore new, unchartered terrains. Interestingly, that which they seek through their explorations is often discovered within themselves.

THE LOVER
The Lover categorizes those who love the pleasures of life and are constantly seeking new experiences. They are passionate and see the beauty in the world around them. They are constantly surrounded by companions since they fear being alone. These individuals may be prone to addiction and fear missing out on experiences in life.

THE DESTROYER
The Destroyer can also be called the Change Agent. These individuals fight the status quo. As they seek change, they will do anything necessary to accomplish their goal. This may put themselves and others in danger. They fear injustice.

THE CREATOR
The Creator is the Artist. These individuals need to create with their hands, be it a beautiful piece of art or a new innovation, as it is through these creations that they better understand the world and themselves.

THE RULER
The Ruler is the Leader. These individuals take charge and inspire others to be the best they can be. They thrive on order and responsibility and are willing to step up when no one else will. They fear chaos.

THE MAGICIAN
The Magician is similar to the Destroyer in that these individuals seek to change the world around them. Unlike the Destroyers, the Magicians will not do it by force but through science and magic. They believe in the Law of Attraction and utilize it for their benefit and that of the world.

THE SAGE
The Sage is similar to the Seeker, in that they both seek the truth. However, rather than having to go out in the world to experience that truth, they look for it within books and meditation. They seek enlightenment and to pass that enlightenment on to others.

THE FOOL OR JESTER
The Fool/Jester is similar to the Lover, as both enjoy life. They play hard and don't always work hard. Everything is fun for the Fool, and in their own way, those belonging to this archetype have found enlightenment.

ONE

REFERENCES

(1) Funk, Cary, and Greg Smith. "'Nones' on the Rise: One-in-Five Adults Have No Religious Affiliation." The Pew Forum on Religion and Public Life, 9 Oct. 2012. Web.

(2) "Distracted Driving Comes with a Cost: Your Life." US Department of Transportation, 10 Apr .2017. Web.

(3) "2010 Census Urban Area Facts." United States Census Bureau, 7 Mar. 2013. Web.

(4) "What Are Electromagnetic Fields: Summary of Health Effects." World Health Organization, 2017. Web.

(5) Brownjohn, James M. W., and Xuahua Zheng. "Discussion of Human Resonant Frequency." *Proc. SPIE* 469.4317 (2001): n. pag. Web.

(6) Lieberman, Matthew D. *Social: Why our Brains are Wired to Connect*. New York: Crown, 2013. Print.

(7) "Feelings Inventory." Center for Nonviolent Communication, 2005. Web.

(8) Pearson, Carol S. *Awakening the Heroes Within: Twelve Archetypes to Help Us Find Ourselves and Transform Our World*. Harper Exilir, 2015. Print.

INDEX

Exercise 1	Getting In Touch With Your Environment	pg 26
Exercise 2	Perceiving the Energy of Your Environment	pg 28
Exercise 3	Emotional Intuition Through Listening	pg 40
Exercise 4	Prayer	pg 58
Exercise 5	Identifying Emotions	pg 95
Exercise 6	Signs from the Universe	pg 97
Exercise 7	Discovering Your Life Theme	pg 106
Exercise 8	Discovering Your Life Lessons	pg 110
Exercise 9	Identifying Your Ego	pg 129

ABOUT THE AUTHOR

Dawn Lynn is a fourth generation intuitive and has had the ability to communicate with Spirit since birth. In 2007, she turned that ability into career. As a medium, teacher and motivational speaker she has empowered thousands of individuals, from every corner of the globe, to live a more purpose driven life through connection to the universe. She lives in Amherst, New York, with her husband, Don, and their daughter, Tierney.

Connect with Dawn at: www.revdawnlynn.com or www.lifeofamedium.com.

www.ingramcontent.com/pod-product-compliance
Lightning Source LLC
Chambersburg PA
CBHW020255030426
42336CB00010B/781